Landmarks of world literature

Marcel Proust

SWANN'S WAY

Landmarks of world literature

General Editor: J. P. Stern

MARCEL PROUST

Swann's Way

SHEILA STERN

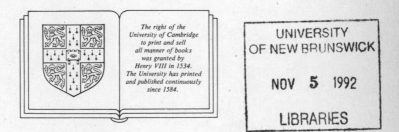

CAMBRIDGE UNIVERSITY PRESS

Cambridge

New York   New Rochelle   Melbourne   Sydney

Published by the Press Syndicate of the University of Cambridge
The Pitt Building, Trumpington Street, Cambridge CB2 1RP
32 East 57th Street, New York, NY 10022, USA
10 Stamford Road, Oakleigh, Melbourne 3166, Australia

First published 1989

Printed in Great Britain at the University Press, Cambridge

British Library cataloguing in publication data
Stern, Sheila
Swann's way; Proust — (Landmarks of world
literature).
1. Fiction in French. Proust, Marcel, 1871–
1922. A la recherche du temps perdu. Du
côté de chez Swann. Critical Studies
I. Title II. Series
843.'912

Library of Congress cataloguing in publication data
Stern, Sheila.
Proust: Swann's way / Sheila Stern.
    p. cm. — (Landmarks of world literature)
Bibliography.
ISBN 0–521–32816–0. ISBN 0–521–31544–1 (pbk.)
1. Proust. Marcel, 1871–1922. Du côté de chez Swann. I. Title.
II. Series.
PQ2631.R63D887 1989
843'.912–dc19   88–31884   CIP

ISBN 0 521 32816 0 hard covers
ISBN 0 521 31544 1 paperback

Contents

Note on the text and its English translations

The page numbers referred to in this book are those of the Bibliothèque de la Pléiade (Gallimard) edition of *A la Recherche du temps perdu*, first published in 1954. It consists of three volumes, each of approximately one thousand pages, containing the following seven parts; the English titles which have become traditional are given alongside.

I	*Du Côté de chez Swann*	*Swann's Way*
II	*A l'Ombre des jeunes filles en fleurs*	*Within a Budding Grove*
III	*Du Côté de Guermantes*	*Guermantes Way*
IV	*Sodome et Gomorrhe*	*Cities of the Plain*
V	*La Prisonnière*	*The Captive*
VI	*Albertine disparue*	*The Fugitive*
VII	*Le Temps retrouvé*	*Time Regained*

Proust tried to dissuade his first English translator, C. K. Scott Moncrieff, from using the title *Remembrance of Things Past*, pointing out that this wording sacrifices the notion of a quest or search. However, the title has firmly established itself and is still used for the revision of Scott Moncrieff's version by Terence Kilmartin, published by Chatto and Windus in 1981 (Penguin Books 1983). All translations given in the text are mine. Since the 65th anniversary of Proust's death in November 1987, copyright in his works has ended and much material relating to his novel has come into the public domain. As this goes to press, some five new editions of the whole or parts of *A la Recherche du temps perdu* are appearing in Paris, one of them a new Pléiade expanded to four volumes by annotations and commentaries. The various forms of the older text, including that of Les Livres de Poche, are adequate for the general reader.

Preface

A guide to *Swann's Way* is irrelevant to readers who have found their own 'way' to Proust. It may appear irreverent as well, since it attempts to deal only with the opening volume of the seven which form the whole of his coherent novel, *A la Recherche du temps perdu*.

The novel is read to the end by a minority of those who make a start on it. The reason for this, apart from its length, may be that in *Swann's Way*, and especially in the first part of it, which editors have agreed to call *Combray*, there are problems resulting from an unfamiliar and original approach; they cease to be obtrusive once this unfamiliarity is overcome. To smooth the path into the first volume, however tentatively, may enable readers to continue with the rest. It was the author's heartfelt intention that the work should be experienced as a totality, and although he obstructed the likelihood of this by the additions he made to the intermediate sections – which, had he lived longer, might have been still more considerable – its true nature can be recognised only by journeying through it to the end. Those who succeed in this are apt to respond to Proust's injunction to start all over again. These are the readers who live with the book, as he lived with it for much of his adult life.

The aim of the present guide is to attend as closely as possible to the language used in the original while keeping in mind the particular questions an English reader is likely to ask; and to avoid misleading generalisations in discussing the text. For nearly sixty years English Proustians have had the benefit of an English rendering to which devoted care was given by the first translators, as it has been by their successors who have improved on it. That these translations are imperfect and unsatisfactory, as most translations are, has not prevented this audience from obtaining an idea of the world-view peculiar to the novel, or from forming their own individual attachment to the work. But to read it in French is a wholly different experience, and for those who find this impossible it may yet be of use to have parts of the French text juxtaposed to a close English version in which faithfulness, rather than elegance, is the principal aim.

Many admirable studies by specialists offer ways of reading Proust in almost inexhaustible variety. Some of them are necessarily too allusive, and assume too complete a familiarity with the work, to be accessible to those reading Proust for the first time. This guide is primarily intended to assist such readers, and is inspired by the vivid recollection of how it felt to make such a beginning.

Chronology

Year			Year	
1880	Marcel suffers a first and violent attack of asthma.		1882	Robert Louis Stevenson – *The New Arabian Nights*.
1884–9	Attends the Lycée Condorcet in Paris.		1883	Paul Bourget – *Essais de psychologie contemporaine*.
Summer 1884	Holidays at Houlgate in Normandy.		1884	J.-K. Huysmans – *A rebours*.
Autumn 1886	A last visit to Illiers.		1888	Anatole France appointed literary editor of *Le Temps*, a republican daily.
1887	Friendship with the thirteen-year-old Marie de Bénardaky.		1889	Paul Bourget – *Le Disciple*.
1889–90	Volunteers for army service, and is stationed at Orléans, where he spends a happy year. The Sunday 'day out' allows Marcel to visit friends in Paris.		1890	Foundation of *Le Mercure de France* by a group of Symbolist writers. Death of the composer César Franck.
1890	Death of Proust's maternal grandmother. September holiday at Cabourg in Normandy; there and at Trouville Proust spends the late summer for many years to come. Leaving the Army in November, enrols as a student of law in Paris.		1891	Foundation of *La Revue Blanche* with a distinguished staff of reviewers including Debussy and Léon Blum.

March 1892	First number of *Le Banquet*, a review founded by Proust and six friends. He frequents the salons of Madeleine Lemaire, Mme Straus (formerly the wife of the composer Bizet), and Mme Arman de Caillavet, through whom he meets Charles Haas and the novelist Anatole France. These two are in part the models for the fictional characters of, respectively, Charles Swann and the writer Bergotte in *A la Recherche du temps perdu*.	
1892		Panama Canal company scandal. Maurice Maeterlinck – *Pelléas et Mélisande*.
March 1893	Last number of *Le Banquet*. Meeting with Robert de Montesquiou with whom Proust will have a long and somewhat stormy friendship, and whose personality suggests traits of the Baron de Charlus in the novel. In this and subsequent years Proust is often a guest in the fashionable and literary salons and enjoys offering lavish hospitality. He also contributes some short sketches to *La Revue blanche*. Graduates in law but persuades his father to let him attend lectures in literature and philosophy, including those of Henri Bergson, recently married to a cousin of Proust's.	
1894	Beginning of the Dreyfus Affair. Like his parents, Proust is pro-Dreyfus from the first.	
1894		Death of Robert Louis Stevenson. Captain Dreyfus of the Ministry of War convicted of espionage for Germany and sent to Devil's Island.

1895   Degree in philosophy.
Holiday in Brittany with the musician
Reynaldo Hahn.

1896   Publication of Proust's *Les Plaisirs et
les jours* by Calmann-Lévy; the volume
includes most of his previously
published work.
There are hints at a novel in progress.
It is eventually to be known as *Jean
Santeuil* but remains unfinished and will
not be published until 1952.

1897   A duel between Proust and Jean
Lorrain over an article on *Les Plaisirs
et les jours*. Each fires two shots but
neither is hurt.
During the years of the Dreyfus Affair
Proust finds himself alienated from
many aristocratic and fashionable
acquaintances who believe Dreyfus
guilty.
In this same period, homosexual
encounters and attachments, some
sordid and some romantic, represent
Proust's secret emotional life.

1897   Doubts become public as to evidence in
Dreyfus trial.

1898   Emile Zola – *J'accuse*; an article in
L'Aurore, a daily paper founded the
previous year to pursue the facts about
Dreyfus, with Clemenceau as political
editor.

1899	Studies Ruskin and begins to translate *Our Fathers Have Told Us* (*La Bible d'Amiens*).	1899–1902		Ministry of Waldeck-Rousseau.
		1899	Dreyfus brought home for re-trial and again condemned, this time for 'treason with extenuating circumstances'.
1900	Two visits to Venice, one with his mother.	1900	Death of Oscar Wilde. Death of Ruskin.
1901	Serious attacks of asthma.	1901	Thomas Mann – *Buddenbrooks*.
1902	Abandons work on *Jean Santeuil*.	1902	André Gide – *L'Immoraliste*. Claude Debussy – *Pelléas et Mélisande*; an opera using Maeterlinck's drama as libretto.
1903	Death of Dr Adrien Proust, taken ill while giving a lecture. Dr Proust had contributed to the study of cholera prevention and to other aspects of public health.		
1904 and 1906	Publication of Proust's translations (on which he had worked with his mother), with his own prefaces and notes, of Ruskin's *Bible of Amiens* and *Sesame and Lilies*.	1904	Separation of Church and State in France.
September 1905	Mme Proust's last illness (at Evian, where Marcel has taken her) and death; she never recovered after losing her husband.	1905	Richard Strauss – *Salome*; an opera from Oscar Wilde's dramatic poem of that name.
December	Proust suffers a nervous collapse and spends six weeks in a clinic at Boulogne.		
1906	In Paris, he moves to an apartment at 102 Boulevard Haussmann. From this time insomnia becomes habitual. He never ceases to mourn his mother.	1906	Dreyfus pardoned and rehabilitated.

1907	Summer at Cabourg, as for the next seven years. Excursions by motor-car with a chauffeur, Alfred Agostinelli, with whom an emotional attachment develops.
1908–9	Proust's literary pastiches of Flaubert, Balzac, etc. appear in *Le Figaro*. He writes the essays which will be *Contre Sainte-Beuve*, remaining unfinished and not published until 1954.
1909	Diaghilev's Ballets Russes perform in Paris. Anatole France – *L'Ile des pingouins*; a satirical novel making use of the Dreyfus case. Maurice Maeterlinck – *L'oiseau bleu (The Bluebird)* – a fairytale drama in the language of Symbolism, with philosophical aspirations; theatrically highly effective.
1910	Rainer Maria Rilke – *The Notebooks of Malte Laurids Brigge*.
1910	Tormented by insomnia, Proust has his room lined with cork to exclude noise. Reads to a friend some pages which form parts of *La Recherche*.
1911	Nobel prize for literature awarded to Maurice Maeterlinck.
1912	Alain-Fournier – *Le Grand Meaulnes*. Anatole France – *Les Dieux ont soif (The Gods are Athirst)*.

1913	Agostinelli becomes Proust's secretary in Paris. Marriage of Proust's driver Odilon Albaret to Céleste Gineste, who will become indispensable to Proust and will take care of him till his death. *La Recherche* 'completed' in three parts, *Swann, Guermantes* and *Le Temps retrouvé*. After many refusals the novel is announced, and *Du Côté de chez Swann* published at the author's expense; the publisher is Bernard Grasset.		
May 1914	Agostinelli, who has broken off relations with Proust and is training as an air-pilot, is killed in a flying accident off Antibes.		
June	Publishers now interested in Proust's novel, and parts of the later volumes come out in the *Nouvelle revue française*.		
July			
August	Grasset closes down temporarily on the outbreak of war and Proust transfers by consent to the *Nouvelle revue française*. Here too publication is delayed by the War, with the result that Proust continues to add to the manuscript.	August 1914	Outbreak of war.
		September 1914	Battle of the Marne.
		1915	Virginia Woolf – *The Voyage Out*.
		1916	Battles of the Somme.

1914–18	Proust's asthmatic attacks are more frequent and he is forced to live as an invalid. His domestic arrangements are disrupted when his servant Nicholas Cottin joins the Army, and Proust spends much time in nursing-homes outside Paris, returning for brief visits. Robert Proust, as an Army doctor, pioneers the establishment of front-line dressing-stations.	1918	Armistice.
November 1918	*A l'Ombre des jeunes filles en fleurs* published.		
1919 June–October	*Pastiches et mélanges* published. The apartment building on the Boulevard Haussmann, where Proust had lived since 1906, is sold by his aunt. He moves house twice, settling in the Rue Hamelin in the care of Céleste Albaret.		
December	The Prix Goncourt awarded to *A l'Ombre des jeunes filles en fleurs*.		
1920	*Du Côté de Guermantes I* published.		
January 1921	The article 'A propos du "style" de Flaubert' appears in the *Nouvelle revue francaise*.	1921	Nobel prize for literature awarded to Anatole France.
April	*Du Côté de Guermantes II* and *Sodome et Gomorrhe I* published.		
June	The article 'A propos de Baudelaire' appears in the *Nouvelle revue francaise*.		

	1922	James Joyce – *Ulysses.* Virginia Woolf – *Jacob's Room.*
April 1922 November	*Sodome et Gomorrhe II* published. Death of Marcel Proust: almost till he died he was at work on additions to the last sections of his novel.	
1923	*La Prisonnière* published. Proust's friend, the writer Jacques Rivière, collaborated with Dr Robert Proust to edit this and the final two volumes of *La Recherche.*	
1925	*Albertine disparue* published – later re-titled *La Fugitive.*	
1927	*Le temps retrouvé.*	
1952	*Jean Santeuil* and	
1954	*Contre Sainte-Beuve* both published by Bernard de Fallois. *A la Recherche du temps perdu* published by Gallimard in the three-volume Pléiade edition prepared by Pierre Clarac and André Ferré.	
1962	Vast family collection of Proust's papers sold by Dr Robert Proust's daughter to the Bibliothèque Nationale.	
1984	The three posthumous volumes (i.e. starting with *la Prisonnière*) re-edited by Jean de Milly and published by Flammarion.	
1987	Flammarion edition completed as copyright expires.	
1987–8	New four-volume Pléiade edition from Gallimard, edited by Jean-Yves Tadié.	

Chapter 1

The matter of *A la Recherche du temps perdu*

It is not easy to summarise a novel which accompanied its author throughout his adult life as a proliferating extension of his experiences in the world and in the imagination. Digression and leisurely speculation are essential to it, there is a wealth of incident but no plot to be outlined; and for all the power of aesthetic and psychological analysis we find in it, the philosophical viewpoint is not explicitly argued by the author but is left to be deduced by the reader.

Proust's title above contains a kind of pun to which he drew attention in a letter to a publisher. If we render it literally as *In Search of Time Lost*, the play on words is fainter than it is in French. The English emphasises the poetic nuance of 'time that has vanished' at the expense of the everyday meaning of 'perdre son temps' − the usual expression for 'to waste one's time'; thus in French the poetic and mundane possibilities are balanced, as they are when Shakespeare's Richard II says, 'I wasted time, and now doth time waste me.'

The title of the first book of the seven-part novel is *Du Côté de chez Swann*, and is explained by its author as deriving from a country speech-habit which has a close parallel in English. Whether the name used is that of a family, a house, a wood or a village, in both languages a topographical reference ('going in the direction of . . .') is intended − as in 'up/down/over Hutchinson's/Tatchbury/Copythorne way' − an allusion to a local landmark. It is, then, clear that when we place level stress on the words 'Swann's way', we do not read them with the intonation their real meaning requires, but it becomes plain, with its secondary resonance, in the text.

At the opening of the novel, a narrator evokes his

childhood and develops ideas about memory. His family have two favourite walks when they are staying at Combray, one that takes them past Tansonville, the property of their friend Charles Swann, towards, but never as far as, Méséglise, and the other beside the river (la Vivonne) in the direction of the estate of Guermantes. So they speak of going 'du côté de chez Swann' or 'du côté de Guermantes'; the two routes are absolutely separate in the child's mind and he is astonished, later in life, to learn that they have a point of intersection and can form one excursion. *Du Côté de chez Swann* is in two main parts, called *Combray* and *Un Amour de Swann*; in the first, that is in the narrator's childhood, Swann appears often, influential as no other figure is outside the family, and acquiring glamour as the boy begins to understand more about his unconventional marriage. *Un Amour de Swann* is entirely devoted to the foregoing history of this marriage, the love-affair that preceded it some years before the events of *Combray* and indeed before the narrator's birth. This preoccupation with Swann, then, is the underlying intimation of the title of the first book, and, similarly, that of the third, *Le Côté de Guermantes*, again recalls the walks near Combray while it traces the narrator's progress in the social world of the ducal family of Guermantes.

We see the events and persons provided by the world as if through a coloured window-glass, which is the narrator's inner life. His perceptions mediate that world for us, and subordinate it. This means that any factual 'outline of events' is of minor importance in our thinking about this work; it is also profoundly untrue, as the outline of the primary material of a lyrical poem is untrue. Yet without the world there would be no perception and nothing to mediate, and it is both paradox and the commonplace of reading Proust that the text conveys physical and mental response to persons and surroundings with an almost unparalleled intensity and in such a way that they enter the reader's subjectivity. It was very much in Proust's mind that the reception of his work would depend to an unusual degree on the individual capacity to accept the way he wrote; modestly but unshakably he was aware of making new demands. The book is a landmark in twentieth-century literature for several reasons, and one of the first to become apparent is that the act of writing and the act of reading are equally its subject-matter. In practice, many who start on it with a feeling of bewilderment come to find, as they go on, that far from imposing an alien set of perceptions, it is only leading them to recognise and explore sensations that are their own.

The linguist Emile Benveniste distinguished, on the basis of verb forms in narrative prose, between '*histoire*' – the story, and '*discours*' – broadly, the way in which the story is told, with authorial generalisations, comment or rhetoric. Literary critics have extended and applied this distinction (now preferring to call the story '*le récit*'). Alternation of *récit* and *discours* in literary texts has been shown to be often very rapid, constant and subtle, far more so than Benveniste's linguistic description suggested. Rarely are the two found interwoven to the extent we have to acknowledge in Proust's writing; and here the distinction between them is perhaps likely to be more helpful as an analogy than, as for other writers, a precise dissecting instrument. The refracting medium of a specific consciousness is always integral to the recital of happenings, and we are reminded of this by many similes (especially in *Combray*) of refraction, of a transparent screen, or of two overlapping surfaces, conveying a modification and renewal of vision or perception. We cannot always separate *récit* and *discours* here – cannot remove the optical glass to look without its mediation at this world – the world will have disappeared with the lens through which we saw it. With this caution in mind we must nevertheless attempt a brief sketch of the material used in the novel as a whole before turning to the closer view of *Swann's Way*.

A man's life is traced from childhood to middle age, and is narrated by himself; no formal introduction is provided. Instead, we hear him beginning to think aloud on the subject of time, memory and his own consciousness, at an indeterminate period in his past, when the habit of insomnia made him particularly aware of the elusive delights of sleep. Soon he begins to recall family holidays in the little town of Combray in northern France, where his mother's cousin, Aunt Léonie, ruled her household from a perpetual sick-bed. This narrator has no name. Unwary critics of the past have called him Proust, while at the other extreme Marcel Muller has recently separated his persona into seven pseudo-selves – the narrator, hero-I, hero-we, intermediary subject, writer, novelist and signatory. Systematically to distinguish between these seven 'voices' might be considered a kind of substitute for reading the novel, or at least as an unwarrantably exhausting game. For the majority of readers it may be enough to bear in mind that some such subdivisions can be made, and that this indicates the delicacy with which we should approach the links between *La Recherche* and its author's own life. His fears that the book would be taken for an autobiography were borne out by some early reactions to *Swann's Way*. That the family setting, the places visited and persons described generally correspond to the facts of Proust's experience is not in doubt, and he was quite forthcoming about identifying the models in real life for some of his characters (incidentally providing a pretext for much uninteresting research). In a later part of the novel, after telling of his feelings when his friend Charles Swann died, the narrator apostrophises this fictional personage and refers to his portrait in a group by the painter James Tissot. This real portrait is that of Charles Haas, a Parisian man-about-town and companion of the great, whom Proust knew and drew upon for his figure of Swann. Thus in a kind of hide-and-seek our frivolous interest in real models is challenged and simultaneously defied with the repeated assurance that everything in the novel is fictitious.

More than most of the writers to whom we might compare him, Proust here and there refers to historically datable events or people of his own lifetime, not only when they loom large in the experience of his characters (as the Dreyfus affair or the 1914 War), but as incidental conversational allusions. The writer closest to Proust in this respect is Balzac, yet there is a great difference in the way they make use of real events, and the effect of Proust's allusiveness is akin to that produced by the writers of social memoirs. The reader's familiarity with minor circumstances of the 'period' is occasionally assumed by the narrator in so easy a manner that our understanding of the book as fiction is subtly undermined and must be voluntarily re-asserted — to say nothing of our need for foot-notes. The first time an assumption of this kind occurs may serve as a slight example. To convey the idea that Swann, unknown to the unpretentious friends he has in Combray, is a valued member of the most exalted society, the narrator lets the reader into a secret. While Aunt Léonie's mother (the narrator's great-aunt) is making use of Swann as an obliging neighbour, she does not know that he has 'perhaps, a letter from Twickenham in his pocket'. We, perhaps, do not know that Twickenham was the residence for most of his life of the Count of Paris, a son of that Louis Philippe who was the last Bourbon King of France; but when the reader has understood that Swann is in correspondence with the exiled prince, the fictional Swann is located in this non-fictional context and must be wrested out of it again by an effort of the imagination.

It might be said that in reading *La Recherche* we have to repeat this process fairly often, not only for Swann, but for the central figure, and that this bears a relation to the various personae whom, as we have said, Marcel Muller identifies. The most important aspect of this is that our acceptance of fictionality is qualified by one peculiarity of Proust's nar-rator: it is that he longs to be a writer, and at the end of his story sees the way to fulfil this longing. Fulfilment is the merging of fictional and non-fictional personae, and this merging has been a potentiality from the beginning. To com-pare Proust's novel for a moment with one by Dickens, we know that David Copperfield's life has some elements of his creator's biography, but in reading *David Copperfield* we never ask ourselves whose voice we are hearing; it is constantly that of a fictional autobiographer. It would not be candid to pretend that *La Recherche* is fully fictional in that sense; but by means of various transferences and suppressions the author frees himself from autobiographical fact for as long as the design of the novel requires it.

We have said that the narrator has no name, but one is usually employed by critics, at least in reference to his younger self; the justication for calling him Marcel is that at a late stage in the novel he is twice so addressed by his mistress, Albertine, and once with the rider (almost as if relenting) 'if we suppose the hero of this work to have the same first name as its author.' It is a grudging concession, but welcome.

A source of complexity in *Combray* is that there seem to be three 'openings' rather than one. The first, headed I, occupying barely six pages, introduces the insomniac remembrancer and centres round the bed he lies in, with glimpses of other rooms where he has slept. The second, unnumbered, selects the Combray bedroom, the earliest he can recall, and describes his childish dread of bedtime, and the magic lantern he had been given to console him. The lantern's pictures (not very comforting perhaps) represented the ancient legend of Geneviève de Brabant and the traitor Golo, sent to murder her. In the next forty pages we learn of the characteristic preoccupations of the household at Combray, and of visits paid to the family by Charles Swann both there and in Paris, where he, and Marcel's parents, lived throughout most of the year — all this in the form in which the adult narrator was long accustomed to remember it. Towards the end of this account he tells of the decisive moment at which these memories were discovered to be no longer related to the truth. They had become a desiccated recital, an oft-told tale as it were, summoned by his 'voluntary memory', suddenly replaced in an accidental revelation by the full recall brought about by 'involuntary memory', that of the senses and not of the intellect. This decisive revelation results from the taste of a cup of tea and a madeleine, a little cake shaped like a shell.

The third opening follows, headed II (p. 48), and starting with the words 'Combray, in the distance . . .' with a new vitality and earnestness; it is clear that we are to share the recaptured fullness of experience. From this point on, childhood, boyhood and early adolescence, mostly during the months of April and May through several years, provide the stuff upon which observation, reflection and self-discovery are superimposed. Incident and characterisation abound, but what would be the framework of a conventional novel – dates, events of practical importance – is subordinated and elided in the course of meditations and impressions; though some of these lead to retrospective explanations very much in the manner of Balzac, and of a kind sedulously avoided by such craftsmen of the novel as Flaubert. *Combray* ends as a circle closing, with 'the raised finger of daylight' outlining the window-curtains, as the night ends, that has passed in recollection – one night, that is, or many nights. As the narrator will tell himself at the end of the last volume. *Time Regained*, the book he has to write will take him 'many nights, perhaps a hundred, perhaps a thousand'. It is the last of many allusive or explicit references to the *Arabian Nights* – the tales of Scheherazade, but also, it seems, to their descendants in Robert Louis Stevenson's *New Arabian Nights*, much admired by Proust, and strangely echoed, as *La Recherche* proceeds, in a variety of nocturnal chases and mysteries.

The second part of *Swann's Way*, which we shall refer to by its French title *Un Amour de Swann* (for fear of confusion with a film called *Swann in Love*) returns the reader to a time before Marcel's birth and is announced as a story he has been told; it is thus narrated in the third person. Chronologically it is straightforward, and allows us to appreciate by contrast the extent of the freedom conferred by first-person narration in *Combray* – a freedom far exceeding what we might anticipate from the practice of earlier first-person narrators. We see the world from Swann's point of view and share fully in his subjectivity, but the absolute intimacy we have known with the narrator is no longer offered, though he puts in an occasional word to connect the adult Parisian world of Swann with that of Combray. The love-affair between Swann and Odette de Crécy, and its social background in the salon of

Mme Verdurin, form patterns which are to be repeated in much of the rest of the novel; many figures now introduced will populate it to its end.

The third and last section of *Swann's Way* is *Noms de pays: le nom*. That is to say, it is the third of the sections to have its own title; but this is a little misleading. In length it almost exactly balances the opening forty-five-page section of *Combray*, which has no separate title and consists of a six-page re-creation of the narrator's nocturnal musings, and a thirty-nine-page account of life at Combray as his 'voluntary memory' used to record it. If this opening section had a title of its own it would be easier to comprehend the plan of *Swann's Way*, which is really in four rather than three parts, arranged thus:

Untitled	Combray II	Un Amour de Swann	Noms de pays: le nom
(6-page 'prelude' + 39 pp.)	(140 pp.)	(233 pp.)	(39 pp. + 6-page 'coda')

The proportional balance of these sections is what Proust wished to emphasise when he wrote in the article 'A propos du "style" de Flaubert' (*Nouvelle revue française*, 1921) that the 'rigorous composition' of *Swann's Way* had been unrecognised even by some very careful readers, no doubt because, as he adds, it is drawn with a very 'wide compass' and the symmetrical parts are distant from each other in the text. *Combray* is itself a title added for convenience of reference by editors, and it did not appear in early issues; the work was published as *Swann's Way*, vols. I and II.

Place-names (*noms de pays*) are the subject of the first few pages of this last section, when we find Marcel living with his parents in Paris after the visits to Combray have ceased because of Léonie's death. A brief evocation of the rooms at the Grand Hôtel de la Plage at Balbec in Normandy, to which, 250 pages later, Marcel will go for a summer holiday with his grandmother, gives the impression of a premonition, a refraction from the future, of a kind we shall often encounter in the course of the book. The major part of this chapter-like section of the book concerns the progress of Marcel's acquaintance in the gardens of the Champs-Elysées with his contemporary Gilberte, Swann's daughter, whom he has hitherto only glimpsed at Combray and with whom he now becomes obsessed. Since her parents fascinate him almost equally, he haunts the Bois de Boulogne in the hope of seeing Mme Swann walking or driving there in the fashionable afternoon procession. This subject leads in to the conclusion of *Noms de pays: le nom*, which is the most audacious and sustained of Proust's dislocations of time – a six-page threnody on the transformation which, since his boyhood, has overtaken the promenaders in the Bois. The most audacious, that is, except for the corresponding six-page nocturnal meditation between sleeping and waking, into which the reader was bewilderingly plunged at the outset of the book, some of the elements of which that reader is by now in a position to locate in their true relation to the narrator's discoveries about himself and the world, while others remain to be recognised like boundary-stones or landmarks as the reading proceeds. This ending of the volume with which we are concerned is problematic. *Swann's Way* was published in 1913, but the appearance of the rest of the book was delayed by the outbreak of war in 1914. Proust took advantage of the enforced respite to rewrite and, above all, expand his manuscript until it far exceeded the proportions of the original plan. *Swann's Way*, already in print, could not be revised; but its author became aware that the strong impression this elegiac ending makes is at variance with the intended conclusion of the novel as a whole in *Time Regained*.

As things turned out the second volume, *A l'Ombre des jeunes filles en fleurs*, known in English as *Within a Budding Grove*, came out only in 1919, when it was awarded the Prix Goncourt. Its first section, entitled in English *Mme Swann at Home*, forms a close sequel to *Swann's Way*. In manner and mood it represents a new, exuberant phase of witty social observation, held in balance with the already familiar preoccupations of the adolescent Marcel – his love for Gilberte, now his frequent companion, his hopes of a literary career, and his anxious desire to please his mother and grandmother. These tentative concerns overlap and conflict with his father's fears for him as the boy becomes a favourite of Swann and

Odette, and through them meets the writer Bergotte, whom he has long admired. The father's prejudice against this novelist is based on the opinion of the retired ambassador and political busybody, M. de Norpois, whose portrait at the outset of the volume is completed by his superb anti-Bergotte monologue. What we seem to be reading here is a pastiche of the nineteenth-century critic Sainte-Beuve confronted with writing of a later time, not unlike that of Proust himself.

The summer in Normandy at Balbec, already talked of even in *Combray*, is the subject of the second and longer part of *Within a Budding Grove*, and is separated by two years from *Mme Swann at Home*. This second part is called *Noms de pays: le pays* — for at this stage the infinitely suggestive power of place-names (*Noms de pays: le nom*) is to yield to actual experience of some of those places. It will not have escaped readers of these pages that while we may feel the lack of chapter-headings or divisions at many points in *La Recherche*, there is rather a plethora of titles for the larger units, some of them provided by the author, and some by editors in difficulties which can be appreciated by glancing through the history of publication in our chronology.

The critic Gérard Genette in his discussion of time in this novel ('*Ordre*', in *Figures III*) points out that from the opening of *Noms de pays: le nom* the narration continues to the end of the whole book without reverting to the original scene and moment from which recollection began. An incident in adult life provides the 'Open, Sesame!' to all subsequent memories, but neither that incident (the madeleine) nor the opening phase of the insomniac in his bed are revisited on the long haul through those memories — it simply passes them by. *A Thousand and One Nights* was, as we have noted, often in Proust's mind when he contemplated his task; but he abandons the narrative logic observed in the setting of Scheherazade's tales by eliding the expected closure of his framework, and never acknowledges the point at which his story overtakes that possible closure.

'In his own way', writes Genette, ' — and probably without even being aware of it — Proust here undermines the most fundamental norms of narration, and anticipates the most disturbing procedures of the modern novel.'

The theme of Marcel's ill-health, which was introduced in *Noms de pays: le nom* is linked with that of the profound communion between him and his grandmother; at Balbec this closeness co-exists with the embarrassment she causes the adolescent by her high-minded simplicity and the contrast it forms with the general tone of the elegant seaside hotel where they are staying. Balbec is the prime example of places that fail to correspond to the images Marcel has accumulated around their names – in this case the expectation of a rocky storm-battered coast with a Gothic church dominating the cliffs. The painful recognition that Balbec is a resort, with carefully tended public gardens and pretty little villas, that the weather is fine and the church not at all near the shore, gives way to delight in the dazzling and ever-changing sea-views and in new acquaintances. One of these is the painter Elstir, whose ideas are used for the exposition of impressionist theory for which this volume is remarkable. The grandmother's old school-friend, Mme de Villeparisis, undergoes a startling mutation in Marcel's mind when she introduces him to her nephew and grandnephew, the Baron de Charlus and Robert de Saint-Loup, and when he learns that all three are members of the Guermantes family whose estate borders Combray. The dowdy, kindly old lady whom Marcel has known for years is transformed in his eyes by the glamour of great lineage. His friendship with Saint-Loup is to become an important theme in the rest of the novel.

But the overriding interest of Balbec for Marcel lies in the girls of the title – *A l'Ombre des jeunes filles en fleurs*, literally *In the Shade of Flowering Girls*. They are a group whose numbers fluctuate, and in which Marcel only gradually distinguishes individuals; at first, on several occasions, they are all seen in a kind of frieze unfurling against the background of the sea. Uncertainly, and then definitively, his preference fixes itself on Albertine.

Driving with Mme de Villeparisis and his grandmother, Marcel sees three trees at Hudimesnil near Balbec and is filled with a delight that brings another reminiscence of Combray — that of a view of church-towers seen from a moving carriage, which then, in his boyhood, had moved him to scribble a descriptive paragraph crammed with similes, and afterwards to burst out singing for joy. This time the presence of the old ladies allows Marcel no leisure to recognise the meaning of the trees, though it seems to convey a summons from involuntary memory. Whenever this sensation visited him, he tells us, he was aware that everything he had experienced since the last occasion was quite unimportant, and that if he could pursue that sensation he might at last 'begin a real life'. Hudimesnil differs from the other moments or places of 'epiphany' recorded in the novel and brought together in the fulfilment of its close, for unlike the others, this remains a mystery and leaves a sadness, '. . . as if I had lost a friend . . . or failed to recognise a god'.

Guermantes Way, the next volume, was published in two parts in 1920 and 1921; the first part of *Sodom and Gomorrha* in 1921, and the second in 1922, not long before Proust's death. *Guermantes Way* begins with the installation of the narrator's family in the apartment which was recommended to them, in the early pages of *Combray*, by Mme de Villeparisis; it is in an annexe of the Guermantes mansion and shares its courtyard. Françoise, the housekeeper from Combray who has become the servant of the 'Paris cousins' (Marcel's parents), is the subject of what is probably the most extended and most delicate portrait of the novel, and much of its vigour resides in these first brilliant pages of *Guermantes Way*. Guermantes is a 'name of power' for Marcel, and he is seized by an obsession with Mme de Guermantes which for the time being displaces his love for Gilberte Swann and the fascination of Albertine. Through Robert de Saint-Loup, social relations are at last established between Marcel and the Duchess, substituting for distant enchantment the opportunity of close observation, which in turn results in disillusionment, for the Duke is boorish and the Duchess, though witty, proves spoiled, spiteful and shallow. Marcel's experience of this new kind of society links his youth with the section of *Swann's Way* in which, at a reception at Mme de Saint-Euverte's, Swann has conversed with his friend, this same Duchess (then Princesse des Laumes, before her husband inherited the ducal title). A long episode in *Guermantes Way I* deals with Marcel's stay at the garrison town of Doncières where Robert is stationed; recalling the Sunday parade of marching conscripts which the child has often seen at Combray, and originating no doubt in Proust's military service of 1889–90 at Orléans, the theme is connected also with that of the 1914 war in *Time Regained*. It gives rise through the consciousness of various characters in the novel to reflections that belong to the philosophy of history.

More important in this respect than the military theme is that of the Dreyfus affair, which dominates part of *Guermantes II*. We should recall that Proust lived through various phases of intense national disarray and dissension – the year of his birth was that in which 20,000 French citizens were killed by French troops in and around Paris during the suppression of the Commune. The Dreyfus scandal, beginning when he was twenty-two, derived some of its bitterness from the struggle between the Catholic, obstinately monarchist conservatism of the higher military ranks and the Republican government they served, which had clung to power since 1871. This scandal split French society as though along a geological fault, and its remote reverberations are said still to be perceptible in certain areas of French life today. In *Jean Santeuil*, a novel Proust worked on roughly from 1896 to 1902, when he abandoned it, the feverishness of contemporary political consciousness breaks through in several episodes and above all in the description of the trial of Captain Alfred Dreyfus, a Jewish officer in the Ministry of War who was condemned on forged evidence for espionage. Like much else in *Jean Santeuil*, this material is elaborated in *La Recherche*, but no longer as a passionately partisan account of historic events. The events, broadly assumed to be familiar to the reader, have been transformed into a set of experiences which have moulded the perceptions of some of the main characters in the novel. Specifically, and not in the form of events but of their psychological consequences for individuals, these experiences are the subject of a long, much-interrupted colloquy between the narrator and Charles Swann at a party in *Guermantes Way II*. Underlying the minutiæ of this 'underside of history' (as Balzac called one of his novels) is the intense concern that informed the long pursuit of the truth, the daily gain or loss of ground, as it was described in *Jean Santeuil*. Like a father speaking of the past to his child, Swann seems to be entrusting a precious lesson to one who will bear witness.

The manner in which such a scene is to be rendered in a novel is obviously of cardinal importance. Swann is himself a Jew, as we have learned incidentally, early in *Combray*, while a first mention is made of Marcel's Jewish school-friend Bloch. Thus the process of shedding a deep-rooted anti-semitic prejudice is not part of Swann's own experience, but he now retails to Marcel the 'confession' made to him on the subject by the Prince de Guermantes. The Prince is the perfect representative of the right-wing Catholic aristocracy, accustomed to think of themselves not as patriots but as the *patria* itself, and his progress from initial unquestioning acceptance of the War Ministry's infallibility, through agonising doubts, to his ultimate certainty of Dreyfus's innocence, stands for the tribulations of all the members of his class who were honest enough to admit the facts, including the dishonour of many gentlemen in every way like themselves.

Swann is ill and fatigued when this scene occurs, and yet refuses to postpone telling his story. This insistence, and the narrator's earnest attention, increase our awareness of the unique place Swann occupies among the figures of the novel. In *Un Amour de Swann* the affair with Odette foreshadows the pattern of the narrator's emotional life; here, in *Guermantes Way*, Swann is a model and a mentor for Marcel in matters of recent history, as he is during the Combray period when he supplies facts connected with art and literature. The conversational means used to convey social history, which could be called gossipy but for the intensity of Swann's manner here, give the flavour of a memoir in the tradition of the writings of the Duc de Saint-Simon, who depicted the age of Louis XIV in similar personal testimonies.

Swann's last appearance forms the conclusion of *Guermantes Way*, a complex scene which has a terrible grandeur. Marcel is the only witness of Swann's unemphatic announcement, to the Duke and Duchess, that he is mortally ill, and of the abominable response they make ('Nonsense! You'll bury us all!') in their anxiety to drive off in time for a particularly glittering party. 'Realistic' consequentiality is avoided: Swann's death occurs 'off-stage', before the beginning of the next volume.

Through M. de Charlus, *Guermantes Way* heralds the predominant subject of *Sodom and Gomorrha*, in allusions and episodes recounted as having been mysterious to Marcel when they first came to his notice. Like Charlus's favourite Balzac, Proust sometimes refers the reader to an impending explanation in a later part of the text, emerging for the purpose, we may feel, from the anonymity in which his narrator usually shields the author, and equating the well-established naïveté of the young Marcel with some assumed guilelessness in that reader. Homosexuality as a hidden undercurrent of society exercises a magnetic force here, strong enough to drag the narrative off course or to threaten the serene equilibrium of matter and manner.

The death of Marcel's grandmother in *Guermantes Way*, and his belated grieving over it in a thirty-page section of *Sodom* entitled *The Intermittences of the Heart*, show us that equilibrium at its most astonishing. *Intermittences* was described by Samuel Beckett in his 1931 monograph as the greatest of Proust's writings. A year has passed since the grandmother's death, and it is his arrival for a second stay at Balbec that brings Marcel's mourning, subdued till then, into anguished life. To read the narrator's account of Marcel's dream about his grandmother is to wonder how it should be possible, in our own century, to set down an archetype of sensibility not recorded before; though it is true that, in a poem called *La Grand'mère*, Gérard de Nerval, who was much loved by Proust, briefly pre-figures this belated mourning in a few simple stanzas.

The pattern of behaviour in love-affairs first established in *Un Amour de Swann* is followed in the course of Marcel's unwary vacillations toward and away from Albertine. What enslaves Marcel, as it had enslaved Swann, is their shared desire, insatiable in a precise sense, to gain control, through knowledge, of all the secret motives and actions of their respective mistresses. Lulled by apparent docility into confidence and boredom, longing to break free, both Swann and Marcel are repeatedly entrapped by the accidental revelation of a new area of mystery and mendacity past or present, and defer the parting already firmly resolved on when they had felt secure. This psychological pattern may suggest something of the immense creative struggle which underlies the presentation of emotional relationships in *La Recherche*. Proust's own experience of such passions (we know) was entirely homosexual, and in transferring that lived experience to a different sphere he may sometimes fail to carry conviction by stressing an extreme of possessiveness which develops under threat, and is more rarely found in socially approved love-affairs.

In the course of *Sodom and Gomorrha* the Verdurins and their little clan reappear in a rented summer residence near Balbec, to which Marcel is welcomed at regular dinner-parties as Swann was welcomed in Paris some twenty years before. This patterning of the narrator's life after Swann's is one of the principal devices by which the perspective of time is extended. Since he is supposed to be already in possession of his mysteriously complete information about Swann's doings, Marcel is able to reflect with astonishment on the persistence of the little clan, and knows its members' characteristics in advance; though he has met only one of them, Dr Cottard, before his first evening with the whole company.

In the first short section of this volume Marcel happens to witness the encounter between Charlus and the tailor Jupien, and succeeds in hearing, though not in seeing, the continuation of the scene after Jupien has locked the door of his workshop in the Guermantes courtyard. As Marcel has placed himself at a staircase window in his parents' apartment to watch for the arrival of the bumble-bee which may pollinate a rare shrub set out for the purpose by the Guermantes servants, the episode takes the form of a long metaphor; for the bumble-bee who arrives is Charlus, and Jupien, on seeing him, instinctively presents the alluring 'display' of a female flower. For Marcel, at least, this casts a new light on the Baron's inclinations and often inexplicable conduct, re-introducing the theme of homosexuality which dominates this volume in particular. At Balbec, in chapter II of *Sodom*, it is Dr Cottard who makes Marcel aware of ambiguities in the behaviour of Albertine's group of friends. Like Swann in his early days with Odette, Marcel is to be pursued throughout his liaison with Albertine by the obsessive fear of her lesbianism.

Through this fear, which deprives him of certainty and baffles his need to 'possess' her by knowledge, Albertine comes to be fatally indispensable to Marcel and is for long months imprisoned in his Paris flat, going out only under surveillance and cross-questioned, when she returns, like a criminal — hence the title of the succeeding volume, *La Prisonnière* — *The Captive*. Albertine's natural duplicity takes on new forms under these pressures, although their shared life has its idyllic moments; Marcel is intent on encouraging his mistress's natural gifts, and they discuss art, literature and the music of Vinteuil in ways that somewhat recall conversations between the writer and his mother in Proust's *Contre Sainte-Beuve*. The presence of Françoise and her inevitable hostility to Albertine form strong links with *Combray*. Once more it must be said that the delineation of Françoise has a delicate vigour, both flexible and consistent, that is, despite its author's contempt for the 'realistic school', a triumphant example of realism — the realism that emerges from a patient and loving study of the human subject.

To keep a prisoner is to be a gaoler and to live in a prison. Little emphasis is laid on Marcel's state of health, though strict rules are enforced on Albertine and Françoise by his need for absolute quiet in the apartment; in *La Prisonnière* he is leading an almost reclusive existence, and there are no more great set pieces at parties or theatres. With Albertine's sudden flight, her death soon after in a riding accident, and the narrator's long mourning, his isolation is relieved only by a few visits from people he has asked to enlighten him about episodes in Albertine's past. *The Fugitive* and the first half of the last volume, *Time Regained*, cannot be considered as finished works — they are work in progress. In the first part of *Time Regained* there occurs a celebrated pastiche of the *Journal* of the Goncourt brothers, followed by a rather feverish set of impressions of Paris in wartime — journalism, fashions, social behaviour and finally the psychology of M. de Charlus are all seen in the uneasy transformations the War has brought about. The gulf that opens between combatants and the civilians they visit in Paris is powerfully evoked in Robert de Saint-Loup's last appearance on leave. Some critics suppose that Charlus and his creator are moving ever closer together at this stage in the novel. The narrator's tracking of the Baron through the Paris black-out, during an air-raid alert, to spy on his flagellation in Jupien's homosexual brothel is the last and the most infernal of a series of such pursuits in *La Recherche*. It recalls the mournful lines about the little country paths at Balbec —

ils me rappelaient que mon sort était de ne poursuivre que des fantômes

they reminded me that it was my fate to pursue only phantoms

in this case perhaps the phantom of a *Doppelgänger*.

Some lengthy footnotes printed with the text bear witness to Proust's expansion of the middle sections of the book; for the purpose of our summary account of the novel as a unity, only the second part of *Time Regained* concerns us.

In this section, which we know to have been completed more or less at the same time as *Combray*, the narrator returns to Paris from one of the sanatoria in which he has spent some of the war years. Finding among his letters an invitation from the Prince de Guermantes to a musical afternoon party, he attends it in the hope of rediscovering something of his own past. Even before entering the house, no longer the ancestral mansion but a magnificent new one, he acknowledges a feeling of pleasure in his outing, though it seems to him frivolous. Literary ambition has been renounced, and he has mourned its hopelessness the very day before, while sitting in the train and contemplating without interest a row of trees half in sun and half in shade, which remind him of his lost ability to perceive a message or a spell in such sights. But in the courtyard of the house, the narrator half-stumbles on an uneven flagstone, and 'as at the moment of tasting the madeleine', he is aware of a mysterious joy and the relief from doubt and anxiety. A sensation of dazzling blueness resolves itself into the vivid recollection of Venice, hitherto merely a series of dull snapshots in his voluntary memory. There, in San Marco, he had missed his footing on a flagstone in a similar way, and the ability to recall Venice has come back to him at the bidding of physical association. Two other instants from the past are evoked during the next few minutes by the senses of hearing and touch; and because his appearance in the drawing-room is delayed, to avoid interrupting the music being performed, the narrator is able to locate and respond to the summons so persistently sounded while he waits in the small library upstairs. Everything is transformed in this sudden favourable conjunction. Even the trees he saw the day before now reveal their power to 'speak' to him that had seemed lost, and the peacock colours of the sea at Balbec long ago are spread out before him. Not only this, but the secret of commanding such moments becomes so clear to him that he is convinced it will not escape again. Thus –

to perceive as quickly as possible the nature of these identical pleasures . . . and then to bring out the lesson I was to derive from them

is the task to be completed at once, and with these words the hortatory or anyway exemplary quality of this least didactic of novels becomes fully apparent. Only memory, permitting us to recognise what we have lived through, is capable of surrounding us with the pure air of paradise – 'for true paradise is the paradise we have lost'. It is scarcely possible, because of the way the world-view of this novel imposes itself on us as we read it, to refuse to recognise that at this point a faith is being offered for our assent.

The work of art, the writing that is to be achieved by self-exploration, begins to define itself in the narrator's mind, and even the books around him in the Guermantes library come to his assistance; the succeeding pages resemble a sequence of notes filled with an urgent confidence in his own writing, which has been denied him till this moment. Art that is subservient to political or social aims, in deference to the parroted outcry against the 'ivory tower'; the school of cinematographic realism; the delusion that the world, things or people possess objectively valid qualities independent of the eye or the heart that observes, judges or loves them — all these are reviewed, seen as irrelevant to the undertaking ahead, and rejected. Yet it is 'the material of my experience, which was to be the material of my book' — the world he has known — that provides the narrator with his inspiration and his confidence. It becomes clear to him, too, that Charles Swann, by his early influence and his practical intervention, has been the begetter at every turn of that experience, and of the perception that will make its interpretation possible.

When the narrator leaves the library and goes into the drawing-room, he is sustained by this revelation in a confrontation with the effects of time which might otherwise seem too terrible to be borne. He already knows of many changes in the lives of those he will see there. The Princesse de Guermantes is dead, and her husband has married the former Mme Verdurin, whose wealth has built this splendid house, and now enables her to dominate the society she affected to despise. Elsewhere he has already encountered the Baron de Charlus in his dotage, but now in a succession of double-takes the narrator sees many others reduced by age to abject caricatures of themselves. A stout though attractive lady seems recognisable as Odette, whose marriage to Swann's old rival Forcheville has at last given her a place in a world that is becoming less exclusive than it was; but the lady turns out to be her daughter Gilberte, who says with a smile, 'You are mistaking me for my mother'. Odette is present too, and the Duc de Guermantes in his old age has fallen violently in love with her; the Duchess pretends indifference to this last infidelity, but her celebrated 'Guermantes wit' has become blurred, raucous, and mechanical.

Throughout this party, the narrator is presented with the task of reconciling his long-held image of each person with the changed appearance he now finds attached to their names. Thus his impression is of being at a masked ball, and he has an impulse to congratulate all these acquaintances on their successful disguises and brilliant mime of ageing. Several incidents bring it home to him that although his hair and moustache are still black, he too is seen to be older; 'You haven't changed a bit', the Duchess tells him, making his heart sink. The solemn lesson soon occurs to him − the precious idea of the book he is now 'carrying' is endangered by his body's frailty, and may never come to life. The ocular demonstration of the effects of Time is as useful to him as the propitious interval in the library; henceforth everything will have to be sacrificed to his task.

When Gilberte brings her beautiful sixteen-year-old daughter to him, the narrator sees her as the living, human counterpart to his new conviction of purpose. The child of Robert de Saint-Loup, who has died in the War, she is both a Swann and a Guermantes; in her the two 'ways' have become one, and time, in this case, has worked unseen to produce not a monster but a masterpiece − it is an allegory which gives hope for the book yet to be written.

The last impression left with the reader is of majesty rather than melancholy. Several times in the account of the Guermantes reception, analogies of height and of depth have suggested the lapse of years lived through by the Prince and his guests. The oldest members of this company, with their cautious, trembling gait, seem to be moving on the dangerous summit of all their eighty years, as though stilts held them up − 'giants, deep in the years' − at an ever-increasing distance from the earth, and doomed suddenly to fall. This image of Time as height, immeasurably extended, allows the narrator to round off the idea he has often used in the same connection, of a dimension proper to human beings but far more elastic and impressive than that we occupy in space.

Thus, too, in *Combray*, the child had apprehended the beloved church of St Hilaire as entirely separate in its essence from the rest of the town:

a building occupying, so to speak, a four-dimensional space – the fourth being that of Time – . . . seeming to conquer and lay claim, not just to a few square yards, but to successive epochs from which it emerged victorious.

Chapter 2

The readers in the book

It is a temptation for critics to suppose their chosen subject an exception to many rules. However, in the matter of his notions about his reading public, Proust is exceptional by any standard. For most of his life he wrote much and published little. His translations of Ruskin (*Sesame and Lilies* [1865], and the *Bible of Amiens* [1884], with prefaces for French readers) were by far the longest works he completed in his first ten years of writing. *Jean Santeuil*, abandoned in 1902, was not published until 1952. The short stories *Les Plaisirs et les jours*, which appeared in 1896, and some sketches, pastiches and articles, brought, from a limited circle, an enthusiastic response for which their author was tremulously grateful. These slight works were all that was available until 1913, when *Swann's Way* was published at the author's expense. The series of chapters, primarily of literary criticism, entitled *Contre Sainte-Beuve*, was probably set aside by 1910, but remained unknown till it was edited by Bernard de Fallois in 1954; the volume includes, in sketched form, some material which found its full development in *La Recherche*, and its publication, forty years after *Swann's Way*, marked a revolution in Proustian studies.

It was thus only in the last eight years of his life that Proust came to believe in the possibility of sympathetic acclaim from a wider, more general reading public. We may justifiably suppose that he wrote to a great extent for himself, and with a few friends in mind; and since the novel uses the subject of reading very freely as a means of conveying the inner life, we may also imagine that he wrote for people much like those who figure in it.

When these characters function in *La Recherche* as readers, they fall into two broad categories, those of Guermantes and those of Combray, the worldly and the unworldly. The first kind make a cult of their own standards of behaviour, and demand instinctively that writers conform to them. Mme de Villeparisis, who belongs by birth to the noble family of Guermantes, provides a striking example when she reproaches the poet Alfred de Vigny with having placed ridiculous emphasis on his own descent from the minor gentry, and the novelist Honoré de Balzac with attempting to depict social circles into which he was never admitted. Hers is the point of view of those exalted circles, and she judges these writers as if she were under imminent threat of their intrusion into her home. Since, as a girl, she frequently glimpsed mid-nineteenth-century celebrities, her literary opinions — like those of the critic Sainte-Beuve — are based on biographical and personal testimony. *Contre Sainte-Beuve*, the essay in which some intellectual aspects of the novel are anticipated, takes its origin from Proust's hostility to this form of literary criticism.

Mme de Villeparisis has several nephews. Of these, the Duc de Guermantes and his cousin Palamède, Baron de Charlus, are both Balzac enthusiasts, though for different reasons. The Duke is inclined to regard Balzac's preoccupation with the Almanach de Gotha — the permanent catalogue of European nobility — as a compliment to his own immense family vanity. The chosen world of the novelist overlaps with his own lineage, and he finds a marvellous if distorting mirror in Balzac's grand imaginary genealogies, estates, passionate intrigues and financial reverses. The Baron de Charlus has a much finer mind than the Duke's, but his attachment to Balzac is in part an emotional self-indulgence. For him, this is above all the writer who found a way to take account of homosexuality as a facet of human life, and to treat the subject with delicate feeling. Not every reader (Charlus is convinced) holds the key to the coded meaning of some scenes in Balzac's *Le Père Goriot*, *Illusions perdues* or *Les Yeux d'or*: to be among the few who do hold this key implies a reciprocal relationship. By virtue of his understanding of these texts, Charlus feels himself understood by them; and in his gratitude he has become an enthusiast for Balzac's other writings too, appreciating the same sensibility in them even where the subject is not as close to his own secrets.

Generally speaking, the Guermantes and their friends have not a literary attitude to literature. It is Charlus, again, who expresses a low estimate of them as readers –

People in my set read nothing and are as ignorant as their footmen.

By the narrator of *La Recherche*, their preferences and judgments are analysed without condescension but with humorous reservations. It is as though he envisaged the different reasons for which these people read as variously valid, and we do not imagine him rejecting any of them as potential readers of the work he might himself produce, though they are not his true readers as he will conceive them. The recognition of the naïve expectations and judgments of such readers as valid is explicit in the introductory section of *Jean Santeuil*, where the elderly fictional author of the work that follows maintains, to the astonishment of his young admirers, that opinions on Balzac should be sought not only among the literati but from

older civil servants, financiers . . . intelligent military men . . . [Balzac's] strength is of a rather material kind . . . it is not by art that he exerts a hold on us. He tries to master us, like life, by a great many things that are bad, and it is life that he resembles.

The member of the Guermantes world who reads most intelligently is Charles Swann, and he only half belongs to that society. In his reading Swann is primarily a scholar, a historian and art-historian who keeps a library of learned works; but in this as in all else he is a dilettante. His attachment to facts often strikes the narrator as strangely exclusive of other beliefs, and has been tentatively ascribed to a modish dislike of expressing strong feelings. Very early in *Combray*, when Swann is first introduced, we read that he was

a man who . . . avoided serious subjects and displayed a very prosaic accuracy . . . even [when the talk was] of artistic matters. Requested . . . to give his opinion, to express his admiration for a picture, he would remain silent almost to the point of incivility, but . . . would make up for it when he could provide factual information about the museum in which it hung or the date when it was painted.

Swann is intermittently engaged in composing a monograph on Vermeer which seems unlikely ever to be completed. His attitude to contemporary novels is that of a connoisseur of style, but underlying it is a kindly tolerance and the notion that they must be of interest mostly to women, including his daughter Gilberte. Finding Marcel, as a boy, reading Bergotte, Swann is very pleased and at once begins to describe the man himself, offering an introduction to him.

The other world in which Swann has his being is that of Combray, and it is here we find Proust's second kind of readers. The narrator's family, and others in Combray, come much closer to that submissive attitude to their reading, unclouded by their own preoccupations, that is the source of bliss for Marcel as a child in Aunt Léonie's garden or in his room. His grandmother, choosing the books she gives him with religious care, and knowing the letters of Mme de Sévigné almost by heart, esteems purity of language and the refined observation of human motives above everything else. An unnamed woman friend of Marcel's mother's in Combray, and the medical specialist Dr du Boulbon in Paris, are among early admirers of Bergotte. What they love in his works is what the boy finds in them: a flow of melody, expressions surviving from an earlier state of the language, the precise placing of others that are simple and familiar; and 'in the sad parts . . . a certain curtness, a tone almost of harshness'. Such sensitivity to cadence and varied tone is remote from the way in which the reading habits of the fashionable world are described, and suggests that the novelist's — Proust's — ideal public is really embodied in the solitary person of Marcel. Immersed in his book with uncritical attention, forgetful of time but aware of the merging of impressions made by the book with those of his physical surroundings, this reading child is the central figure of the first half of *Swann's Way*.

In the final section of *La Recherche* Proust tells us, through his narrator, who by this time is about to 'become' the novel's author, something of the readers for whom he hoped to write; given the history of the book, it is an act of faith even to describe them:

To return to myself, I was thinking more modestly of my book, and it would in fact be inaccurate to say, referring to those who would read it, 'of my readers'. For, as I thought, they would not be my readers, but the readers of their own selves, my book being only a kind of magnifying glasses like those the optician at Combray used to offer to a customer; my book, thanks to which I would provide them with the means of reading in themselves. So that I would not expect them to praise or blame me, but only to tell me if I have got it right, if the words they are reading in themselves are really those I have written — the possible divergencies on this point being, anyway, not always attributable to my error, but sometimes to the reader's eyes not being of the kind for which my book would be appropriate for reading in oneself aright.

This is indeed a modest statement, and at the same time the immense, proud expectation of a reading public fit to be 'read' by the book in their turn.

What makes the Guermantes set supremely interesting *as readers* is the discovery, only available since the publication of *Contre Sainte-Beuve* in 1954, that Proust's idea of them as part of his novelistic material actually took shape while he wrote his counter-attack on Sainte-Beuve's criticisms of Balzac.

In November 1908, in a letter to his friend Georges de Lauris, Proust refers to his wish to write of Saint-Beuve, and asks for advice. Should it be a conventional article, or should he set his remarks in a 'frame', introduced by his mother's waking him in the morning, and by their dialogue? This second form was finally chosen, and with it, as regards the introduction, the first-person narration. A whole set of half-fictional, half-autobiographical details seem to have imposed themselves, later sections ('La Méthode de Sainte-Beuve' in particular) are in the form of straightforward articles, and others again, such as 'Le Balzac de M. de Guermantes' take on the dimension of discursive social portraiture. As a whole, the work provides the transitional link between criticism and fiction, and even 'La Méthode de Sainte-Beuve' has an unfinished foreword of a personal nature, expressing the author's fear that indolence and ill-health will prevent his saying what only he has it in him to say. Christ's commandment 'Work while you still have light' is quoted here, anticipating a dominant theme in *La Recherche*. Three of the essays illustrate Sainte-Beuve's failure to understand his contemporaries Nerval, Balzac and Baudelaire (to the last of whom Sainte-Beuve also behaved abominably), and together these essays form a sustained attack on the most influential literary pundit of the French nineteenth century.

In *Contre Sainte-Beuve* the imaginary though typical readers of Balzac figure as the Count and Marquis de Guermantes (they will be Duke and Prince in the novel), but their visitor, the narrator, goes on to describe the Countess too and the intimates of her salon, their speech-habits and mannerisms, in what has ceased to be a discussion of Balzac and become a serious pastiche of his writing. In a few pages we have the nucleus of *Guermantes Way*, a social world whose inhabitants have irresistibly emerged, as it were obliquely, from the contemplation not of Balzac's works but of those who read him.

Chapter 3

Combray

The book and the bed

Proust's novel begins and ends with the word 'time': the first word 'Longtemps' emphasised by the succeeding comma, the last, 'Temps' by its capital letter. In the first paragraphs references to divisions or lapses of time proliferate – 'de bonne heure' (early); 'quelques secondes' (a few seconds); 'une existence antérieure' (a previous existence) – and then gradually become less insistent. These words provide a steadying background to a first-person voice evoking the state of semi-wakefulness, on the way into or out of sleep, which is a universal experience; a book, just laid aside, conditions an initial phase of deluded rationality – 'it seemed to me I was what was being discussed in the book: a church, a quartet . . .' – but the chief components of that state are fleeting physical sensations and even more elusive attempts at thought. The movement towards fuller consciousness demands a revaluation of phenomena misinterpreted seconds before, and to effect this the mind must wait on memory, which sleeps more soundly than all its other functions:

comme j'ignorais où je me trouvais, je ne savais même pas au premier instant qui j'étais.

as I had no idea where I was, I did not even know, for a moment, who I was.

In the words of a much later part of the novel, a reminiscence and expansion of these first pages:

Alors de ces sommeils profonds on s'éveille . . . ne sachant qui on est, n'étant personne, neuf, le cerveau . . . vidé de ce passé qui était la vie jusque-là. (*Sodome et Gomorrhe II*, p. 162)

29

From this deep sleep we awake . . . not knowing who we are, as nobody, anew . . . the brain emptied of that past which was our life till then.

In the first and second paragraphs of *Swann's Way*, through the narrator's inward eye, and not summoned by his memory so much as by his surroundings — a distant train-whistle, his watch showing midnight — we glimpse a figure or figures whose relation to him is not clear, and whom we must wait a long time, in our reading, to identify as himself, at later stages of the novel, but seen from a great distance, as he will never, in those stages, be seen again. These are the first intimations of the need to read this work more than once, and not always straight through, which imposes itself at many points, and unmistakably when we reach the last page.

The fifth paragraph of *Combray* begins with the words:

Un homme qui dort tient en cercle autour de lui le fil des heures, l'ordre des années et des mondes.

A man asleep holds about him in a circle the threaded hours, the order of the years and the worlds.

There is a note of solemnity and even of grandeur here, and the image of the circle is Dantesque, the diagram of a secret but familiar cosmos. A kind of free commentary, generalising from the sleeper's experience and returning to its particularity, alternates with and clarifies his subjective confusions. But most of this section describes the experience in the first person, as intimate notation. Stripped of his waking attributes, the sleeper's consciousness is one with that of animals or of primal man, and to return to his own time and place he must pass through dizzying seconds in which a sophisticated civilisation reassembles itself, until he is deposited in its midst by the aid first of physical and then of mental memory: the walls and furniture of his room whirling silently about him in the dark, as they take the forms of various rooms where he has slept in the past, before 'the good angel of certainty' restores everything to the present, and to the space that belongs to that present.

Paradoxically, attention is being lavished on a state of

near-oblivion universally familiar as defying any effort of attention whatsoever, a passageway or underside of our experience that had seemed to countless generations of writers incapable or unworthy of being examined or articulated. Speculative riches and astonishment are uncovered in an area of common knowledge of the world usually passed over with impatience. That habitual dismissal begins to seem curiously culpable, a form of sloth and possibly of cowardice − sloth in an almost physical sense, the absence of observation of what lacks colour and sound; and, at a deeper level, fear − a turning away from the unknowable that we associate with the blurring of our responses, with death. There is no mention of fear in this part of the text, yet 'certainty' is greeted as a good angel when it is achieved; wit − the whirling walls, the procession of new inventions such as oil-lamps and turned-down shirt-collars into the caveman's bare existence − comes to validate the acceptance of vertigo and loss of identity; but again, to balance our reading of these first paragraphs, we need their echo in *Sodom and Gomorrha II*:

J'etais effrayé . . . de penser que ce rêve avait eu la netteté de la connaissance. La connaissance aurait-elle, réciproquement, l'irréalité du rêve?   (*Sodome et Gomorrhe* II, p. 167)

But I felt afraid at the thought that this dream had had the distinctness of consciousness. Could consciousness, conversely, have the unreality of a dream?

These few introductory pages end with allusions to some of those once-familiar rooms which memory has recreated in the course of the awakening − 'I was in the country at the house of my grandfather, dead these many years . . . in my room at Mme de Saint-Loup's' − and to places and ways of life he then lies awake remembering. Those two houses are separated by half his lifetime, and the reader will not be in a position to identify Mme de Saint-Loup with Gilberte Swann until near the end of the novel. The time in which these drowsy evenings, fitful wakings and musings occur is the period of adult life in which the book began, only characterised by the word 'Longtemps'. It is a span which comes to a provisional end with the words 'Il y avait bien des années . . .' some forty pages later, at the opening of the episode of the madeleine and its revelation of involuntary memory. At the end of *Combray* we are reminded that the intervening reminiscences, from what we have called 'the third opening', headed II, originate in that revelation, and consequently belong to a later phase of the same span of time:

Thus until morning I would often go on thinking of the time at Combray . . . and of so many other days, too, whose image had been restored to me more recently by the taste . . . of a cup of tea.

It must be said that the reason for beginning the novel with the narrator's somnolence is at first not likely to be clear to the reader. A Monsieur Humblot, who reported on the manuscript of *Swann's Way* for the Paris publisher Ollendorf, wrote that he could not understand how the author could spend thirty pages (actually six) describing himself tossing and turning in bed before falling asleep. Many tens of thousands of critical words later, this reaction is still by no means unusual. Readers less impatient than M. Humblot may be carried onward, even overwhelmed by the effect of surprise and by what at this stage we must simply call the charm of the writing. Others may feel that patience and submissiveness are being exacted in an excessive degree. Certainly a demand is being made of us, and its purpose is not yet clear. It is the demand that we consider the process of writing as an integral and articulated part of the book, not just as the mechanical means by which it has become available to us.

In the opening paragraph we were given a glimpse of the narrator letting a book slip from his hand as he drowsed off, and briefly aware of his own hallucinatory identity with the book's subject − a church, a quartet, the rivalry between Francis I and Charles V. As *Combray* closes, the consciousness of the man in bed is concerned with himself as the central subject in a more definite way: he is no longer 'in' a work by someone else's hand, but ranging through his own mind, which is to say his memory. He is still in the passive state proper to a reader, but the 'book' he reads is himself. The ultimate outcome of his passivity will be the accomplish-

ment of a task, when this new 'book' is no longer his alone
to read, but his to write.

Memory and the will

In the drowsiness and the will-less inattention we have spoken
of we see a facet of common experience that belongs to no
pattern of story telling, and which, though it does not exclude
them, is not under the control of intellectual processes. This
experience derives from physical perceptions and remains in
contact with them during the exploration of the mental
dynamism they call forth. In particular, the value of the floating
condition of half-wakefulness is plain in the emphasis that is
placed on the role of memory, first re-establishing the body's
identity and then, unbidden, bringing discrete glimpses of the
present and the past, which nonetheless form a coherent picture by virtue of the physical presence, at their centre, of the
sleeper and the bed.

The distinction between voluntary and involuntary memory
introduced a little further on in *Combray* is of importance
throughout *La Recherche*, and Proust refers to it as the basis
of his writing. But it would be wrong to suppose that he
recognises no other varieties of memory, or that every time
the narrator uses words relating to memory it is possible to
classify this use as one or the other of these two kinds. Certainly the operation of the mind in the first pages falls into
the general class of the involuntary; but it does so without the
force the narrator is going to attach to involuntary memory
in his grand distinction, for the narrator's lethargy limits the
effect of memory, and his reception of its messages has so far
been entirely passive. This appears paradoxical, since passivity
and unawareness must be admitted as the precondition for the
visitations of involuntary memory, but there is another essential factor which is to be demonstrated, rather than stressed,
by the manner in which these visitations develop and take on
their true significance. This essential factor is the mind's
readiness to respond to the unanticipated message by changing its own course: passivity vanishes, and all the faculties

are concentrated in willed attention, a static energy at the opposite pole from helpless lethargy.

A Combray, tous les jours dès la fin de l'après-midi . . . (p. 9)

At Combray, every day from late afternoon on . . .

Thus begins the 'second opening', the illustration for our present purpose of the narrator's voluntary memory of his childhood holidays. The pages (9–43) that introduce the household at Combray, under the guise in which the narrator long recalled it, have a melancholy cast, for what he chiefly remembered was his childhood fear of the inevitable bedtime. The thought of being separated from his mother then over-shadowed each afternoon with an obsessive foreknowledge of loss. Vignettes of members of his large and loving family, their servant Françoise and their frequent visitor Charles Swann, are interwoven with the child's mute anguish, though it takes the form only of brief allusions, like a musical motif, while the narrator is acquainting us with information he gained later or comments on as an adult, and already touching on major themes of the novel. It is not always properly acknowledged, in the solemnity of the critical approach, that there is as much comedy as sorrow in this section of the book, though we have used the word 'melan-choly', and though the section ends with an emotional scene of extraordinary power. The great-aunts Flora and Céline, who have studied the piano with the musician Vinteuil and who almost entirely disappear from the novel after this, are unforgettable examples of the belief that it is vulgar to express oneself lucidly. Charles Swann's father, who has died before Marcel's birth, is commemorated in a poignant anecdote of inter-mittent amnesia which has become part of Marcel's family's comic lore. It is mostly Marcel's grandfather, less often his father, who perceives humorous aspects of behaviour; the child who 'sees the joke' through their eyes, and the adult narrator who records it, are not easy to distinguish here because their voices merge in one sacred to this shared repertoire.

Though Swann's frequent appearance as a guest at dinner regularly intensifies Marcel's anxiety, because it means his mother will not leave the table to kiss him goodnight in his room, it is on one particular evening that a crisis is reached. Defying the rules, Marcel waits on the stairs till the late hour of her own bedtime, sustained by his obsession but in terror of his father's anger. The outcome is the unhoped-for, decisive capitulation of the father in the face of this distress — he suggests that his wife should spend the night in the child's room.

The paragraph in *Combray* describing this incident is used by Erich Auerbach in the conclusion of his book *Mimesis*. With its intense particularity of recollection — the father in his white nightshirt and coloured headscarf, the candle he holds lighting up the staircase wall — and its interweaving of these visual details with a later time as well as with the child's associative perception in his own time (his father is long since dead, the staircase has ceased to exist, his father's gesture reminds Marcel of Abraham in an engraving after Benozzo Gozzoli which Swann has given him) — the extract illustrates, according to Auerbach, 'the reflection of multiple consciousness'. The principal subject of this last chapter of *Mimesis*, entitled 'The brown stocking', is Virginia Woolf's evocation of Mrs Ramsay's own awareness at a particular moment (while she measures the stocking she is knitting against her little boy's leg) together with speculations about her inner self and her history in the minds of unnamed and named acquaintances who have seen on her face, at other times, the same unfathomable sadness it has at this moment. The two texts are used to point the way forward from the literature of realism which is the subject of *Mimesis*, and they are juxtaposed, not compared. For our purpose the juxtaposition underlines, in the Proust passage, the function of the first-person narration, which can command the recollection of a mental state with its physical conditions, together with a shift to the writer's situation in his own present time, the time in which his hand rests upon the paper of his manuscript, while his mind is occupied by the awareness of bereavement arising from the scene just described. This unexpected yet gentle move (beginning 'Il y a bien des années de cela', p. 37 — 'Many years have passed since then'), which also admits us into a timeless 'now' with the word 'maintenant' sixteen lines on, is one that is not available to a third-person narrator however omniscient. Mrs Ramsay's consciousness and those of her friends are transparent to her creator, but are fixed within the temporal framework of a story, while Marcel's is one with that of the adult narrator, here forming a seamless authorial self we can hardly presume to analyse into distinct parts. At such moments in this narrative, rare as they will prove, it is well to keep in mind the whole of Proust's often partially-quoted comment on his writing — '[le] narrateur qui dit "je", et qui n'est pas toujours moi' — 'the narrator who says "I" and who is *not always* myself' (italics mine). That narrator asserts his identity with the author as the scene concludes:

Such moments will never be possible for me again. But for some time now, if I listen attentively, I have been able to hear again quite clearly those sobs I had the strength to stifle in my father's presence, and which broke out afresh only when I was alone with mama. In reality they have never ceased; and it is only because life is growing quieter around me now that I hear them again, like convent bells so completely blotted out by the noises of the city during the day that you think they have stopped ringing, but which start to sound again in the silence of evening.

Memory, here, is a recurring mental pattern, a haunting, neither voluntary nor involuntary.

Contradictory emotions are aroused in Marcel by this scene, with its explicit parental admission that he is suffering from a nervous disturbance he cannot control; his mother's increased anxiety about him causes him to feel guilty, while he enjoys the consequent routing of the unsympathetic Françoise. Critics incline to assimilate these reactions to patterns of behaviour they discern in the novel as a whole; thus Valerie Minogue, in her book on *Du Côté de chez Swann* (1973), tells us that Marcel's disobedience in waiting up for his mother is 'an apparently trivial act [which] irretrievably marked his life with a sense of guilt and failure'. This implausible statement ignores the delicately analysed complexity in which joy ultimately prevails — 'my remorse was pacified, and I yielded to the delight of having my mother with me for that night'. Marcel's lasting sense of guilt in relation to his mother is composed of many elements yet to be made plain. Another writer, Roger Shattuck in his *Proust* of 1974, equates the child's tearful welcoming of his heart's desire with later episodes in which disappointment attends the granting of Marcel's fervent wishes, but this is not a comparable case. As with the various kinds of memory, we should beware of assigning each response, within the rather narrow range of worldly experience this novel uses, to some ready-made category which criticism has established as 'Proustian'. If such a procedure were justified in the interpretation of this very long novel, the reader of it might well complain of tedium instead of being surprised by unpredictable variety. There is a realism in the presentation of the child here which forbids our making of him a little Faust, insisting on the renewal of desire even as it is fulfilled; and Marcel will be, throughout the novel, capable on occasion of accepting and rejoicing in the moment that is passing.

Till this point, it will be remembered, all we are told of Combray is what has long been available to the narrator's memory when his thoughts turned to his childhood; and in a brilliant résumé based on the metaphor of the theatre, these reminiscences are said to have had as their setting only

the bare essentials of scenery for the drama of my undressing; as though Combray had consisted only of two storeys linked by a slender staircase, and as though the time there had always been seven o'clock in the evening.

No stranger's question, the narrator tells us, could have helped him to retrieve his living past; the part of memory that is governed by intelligence might have provided factual information, but nothing of the essence. A brief reference to Celtic stories of souls imprisoned in trees or in animals illustrates the idea that we depend upon the lucky chance of encountering, before we die, the unsuspected object in which there lie imprisoned the sensations that will reveal our past to us as intelligence cannot do. Now, at last, the celebrated incident of the morsel of cake crumbled in a spoonful of tea releases the narrator's 'involuntary', instinctual memory through the power of long-forgotten physical experience.

The revelation is at first so entirely bound up in the sense of taste that it evades thought: 'a delicious pleasure' and the falling away of the preceding fatigue and discouragement are all that the mind is aware of. The effort to grasp the process rationally is described in uncharacteristically staccato sentences in the historic present tense:

this unknown condition . . . I set out to make it reappear. I go back in my thoughts to the moment when I took the first spoonful of tea. The same condition returns with no new light upon it.

Even covering his ears to exclude sound, the narrator empties his mind and 'confronts' it with the still recent taste:

et je sens tressaillir en moi quelque chose qui se déplace, voudrait s'élever, quelque chose qu'on aurait désancré, à une grande profondeur; je ne sais ce que c'est, mais cela monte lentement; j'éprouve la résistance et j'entends la rumeur des distances traversées. (p.46)

and I feel stirring in me something that is moving, trying to rise, something just loosed from its moorings, at a great depth; I do not know what it is, but it is slowly making its way upward; I can feel the resistance, and hear the echoing, of the distances it has to travel.

Starting from the initial sensation, the intellectual effort is resumed ten times or more, and each time 'the indolence or cowardice that diverts us from any difficult undertaking' (the same indolence and cowardice we have mentioned, which the narrator often complains of as his besetting sins) counsel him to abandon the task and return to his thoughts of the day just past and that to come. In the end the memory is recaptured: the taste is that of the tea and the madeleine his Aunt Léonie would offer him on Sundays at Combray, when he went to wish her good morning in her bedroom; and the memory this taste has restored to him is of the whole temporal and spatial experience of Combray which he had been incapable of recalling voluntarily.

Baudelaire, in his poem 'Le Flacon', makes use of a comparable sensory arousal in a series of dense and lurid images: the memory of a woman arises from a scent sealed in an old phial. In this poem, the resurgence of the past is violently unwelcome to the unwary violator of the seal; in a hand-to-hand struggle with the subconscious, the mind is 'terrassé' – thrown down on the brink of the abyss in which the dead self lies, 'a stinking Lazarus' ready to be brought back to life by the scent. This is at the opposite pole from the arduous entreating of memory in Proust's novel, and there is in the poem no interval between the originating sensation and the recognition. Yet the intimate linking of physicality with memory in Baudelaire was one of Proust's chief reasons for admiring him, and it is no doubt this poem that Samuel Beckett has in mind in his discussion of involuntary memory in Proust when he says it involves 'not merely the past object, but the Lazarus that it charmed or tortured'. In his brilliant, brief, idiosyncratic guide to Proust, published in 1931, Beckett seems not to accept the importance of the will in the episode we have just been concerned with. He finds the notion of passivity so powerful that, in taking over for a moment Proust's image of the 'depths' from which the memory of Aunt Léonie's room is dredged up, he writes of the 'diver' sent down in search of it, and adds: 'Proust calls him [the diver] involuntary memory'. But the diver, surely, is an agent, that is, *acting* on a hint, on glimpsed information; not passive but alert, strenuously trying to locate: the diver is the will.

The reader's role

Even in the midst of the startlingly subjective 'overture' to *Combray*, the words 'a man asleep', and later 'Perhaps the immobility of things about us . . .' indicate an appeal to our own experience. The first person singular alternates with the plural form to ensure our recognising that the narrator's reflections are taking on the universalising manner of the philosopher, the critic and the psychologist. This manner, though still unemphatic, becomes more apparent in the earnestness of the pages we have just discussed, in which the discovery of involuntary memory is made.

The universalising manner is nothing new in the novel; in

fact it is its suppression that is a characteristic of modern fiction since Flaubert. Writers before and since his time habitually assume or demand our assent to moral judgments or psychological interpretations, though the word 'unemphatic' we have just used might be inappropriate to some of them. George Eliot, whose *Mill on the Floss* Proust more than once named as the novel he loved best, provides, early in that work, an example of such a demand when she expresses as a rhetorical question her idea of there being two kinds of memory:

We have all of us sobbed so piteously . . . but we can no longer recall the poignancy of that moment and weep over it. . . . Is there anyone who can recover the experience of his childhood, not merely with a memory of what he did and what happened to him . . . but with an intimate penetration, a revived consciousness of what he felt then?

Balzac often addresses similarly imperious questions to the reader, though he commands a wide range of subtler appeals for our collaboration. But these appeals are formalized compared with Proust's manner; they represent a conscious break between *discours* and *récit*, a pause for moralising, which is good for us, in the midst of narration, which is to entertain us. As we have already said (p. 3 above), Proust's writing tends to merge these forms, distinct in other authors, and draw us in to share his intimate inquiry into, and response to, impressions assumed to be ours as well as his own, not to judge or interpret from the outside. This intimacy has the effect of an extension of the writing self, which accommodates us, while we read, like an *alter ego*. We are given the authority to measure our sensibility, rather than our beliefs, against the narrator's own. An earlier writer who comes to mind as a forerunner in this respect is Walter Pater, whom Proust admired. Between *Combray* and some of Pater's sketches, such as *The Child in the House*, there are striking resemblances of primary material, but also a similarity in the easy assumption of confidence in the reader's response to the writer, as though the various barriers normally separating them had melted away.

'Combray takes on form and solidity' — the third opening

Combray, de loin, à dix lieues à la ronde, vu du chemin de fer quand nous y arrivions la dernière semaine avant Pâques, ce n'était qu'une église résumant la ville, la représentant, parlant d'elle et pour elle aux lointains, et quand on approchait, tenant serrés autour de sa haute mante sombre, en plein champ, contre le vent, comme une pastoure ses brebis, les dos laineux et gris des maisons rassemblées qu'un reste de remparts du moyen âge cernait çà et là d'un trait aussi parfaitement circulaire qu'une petite ville dans un tableau de primitif.   (p. 58)

Combray in the distance, from twenty miles away all round, seen from the train by which we used to arrive there the week before Easter, was nothing but a church epitomising the town, representing it, telling of it and speaking for it to far-off places, and, on a nearer view, keeping close about its high dark cloak, in the open field, against the wind, like a shepherdess her sheep, the woolly grey backs of the huddled houses, edged here and there by remains of mediæval ramparts with an outline as perfectly circular as that of a little town in a painting by a primitive artist.

As soon as the narrator has regained the fullness of his recollection of Combray, he embarks on his account of it as though doubling back to the point in the text which started in a similar way — 'A Combray . . .', and which we now know to have been concerned with the partial memory only, dictated and dominated by his childhood anxiety. The mental picture of Aunt Léonie's house as —

a kind of lit-up panel picked out amidst vague shadows . . . the little sitting-room, the dining-room, the opening of the dark garden-path by which M. Swann would arrive . . . the staircase . . . and, at the top, my bedroom with . . . the glass-paned door for mamma's entrance

— her entrance, that is, on the stage of the nightly drama, which was all he could voluntarily recall — this picture is now to be filled out, and has become a whole house with the varied lighting, sounds and fragrances of times of day other than 'seven in the evening'; a house in a town full of people, gardens and flowers, with a few shops, and the church of St Hilaire as its centre.

The sentence quoted above ('Combray in the distance . . .') dispels any earlier impression that the novel will provide only such troubled or distorted refractions of real objects and people as that 'lit-up panel'. The simile of the cloaked shepherdess is the type of many images by which the narrator endows architecture and natural forms with a human presence, and suggests the affection, at times the passion, of his response to them. The comparison of the view with that of a town in a particular kind of painting also foreshadows something of the role of the visual arts in the narrator's sensibility, and in that of Swann. In spite of these elements of intellectualisation, or rather with their aid, the description of Combray here and in the following sentences has the 'form and solidity' promised just before, it is continually rendered transparent or multi-dimensional by the narrator's inter-polated re-creations of his own sense-impressions as, follow-ing the traditional habit of the reader of a realistic work of fiction, we build up our own notion of Combray. Although we learn that the narrow streets with gables and projections made the town somewhat dark and grey, a closer view of the interior setting makes us aware that among the things formerly hidden by the curtain of oblivion was the general source of light: Combray recaptured is now full of sunshine.

The sophisticated and melancholy adult who has been our informant thus far is revealing his capacity for conveying a state of consciousness that is expansive and securely at home in the world in spite of its vulnerability. The change in mood corresponds to the change in Combray itself as it 'takes on form and solidity'. The hopelessness and fatigue, part of the narrator's given situation just before the revelation of the madeleine, seem now to belong to, and to shape, the earlier image of his childhood as overshadowed by a neurasthenic obsession − the image he owed to voluntary memory alone, and which is now condemned as false. With this perspective we look back at the speculative liberty of the 'first opening', its virtuoso evocation of sensuous joy in different rooms and seasons of the year, as having been engulfed by tragic awareness when Golo, in the legend, started his staccato course across the yellow field at the 'second opening'. As the colours of the magic lantern flickered over the real objects in the room, so the remembered world has been stained with the colour of the child's unmitigated intuition of grief and parting – coloured strongly enough to vitiate and shrink everything but the intuition itself. Throughout the rest of *Combray* – despite the reiteration, at long intervals, of the almost musical note of the adult's regret for what is lost, and of the child's premonitory dread of evening – it is, from the 'third opening' on, a mood of serene and lively recollection that is communicated.

This duality of mood we will eventually recognise as the extended illustration of a self-analytical comment which occurs in the final paragraphs of *Combray*. The carefree pleasure of the long walk towards Guermantes ends with the sight of the last farm on the way home: 'suddenly my heart would begin to throb', because just at that point the sunset light reminds Marcel of the lateness of the hour, which means he will be dismissed to bed soon after getting home, and his mother's 'goodnight' will be briefly given at the dinner-table.

La zone de tristesse où je venais d'entrer était aussi distincte de la zone où je m'élançais avec joie, il y avait un moment encore, que dans certains ciels une bande rose, est séparée comme par une ligne d'une bande verte ou d'une bande noire. On voit un oiseau voler dans le rose, il va en atteindre la fin, il touche presque au noir, puis il y est entré.   (p. 183)

The zone of sadness I had just entered was as distinct from the zone in which I had been joyfully running along, only a moment before, as is the separation in some skies, like a line between a band of pink and a band of green or black. A bird is seen flying in the pink colour, it has nearly reached the edge, is about to touch the black, then disappears in it.

We may note here (anticipating a longer discussion of the subject below, pp. 88–89) that the image of happiness and misery provided by the colours of sunset, and of the child represented by the bird, is an example of the tendency to metonymy in metaphor strongly characteristic of some sections of *La Recherche* and uncommon in others. Suggested by the circumstances of the walk, the terms of the metaphor are

the opposite of 'far-fetched'; yet there is no doubt that it is
a true metaphor.

In spite of this black evening sadness, Marcel would rise
happy, next morning, and never think that the day would
bring back the hour when he must leave his mother; and thus
it is that on the Guermantes way he learns

> to distinguish between these states of mind which alternate in me
> . . . even to the point of dividing each day in two . . . side by side,
> but so separate from each other, so devoid of any communicating
> link, that I can no longer understand, nor even imagine, in the one
> state, what I have wished for, or feared, or managed to achieve, in
> the other.

This energetic statement of duality helps us to understand
that the joy of 'recovering' Combray is twofold. Besides the
successful foray into the past, the repossession of a time that
was lost, there is the joyfulness of that time itself – a
joyfulness which could co-exist with the foreboding of loss
and was capable of obliterating it. The capacity for immersion in one mood to the total forgetfulness of the other
remains characteristic of the narrator's adult self, and at a
great many points in *La Recherche* the reader will be reminded
of it.

Announced as a discovery with the words 'j'ai appris' (I
learned), this, with other acquired insights, allows us to
recognise how this novel is akin to the traditional
'Bildungsroman' – the story of an apprenticeship in life.
Here, at the end of *Combray*, the insight casts a backward
light, but it is one that does not always illuminate the reading
given to this volume by critics. That of Samuel Beckett, for
instance, conveys with poetic force the idea of a pall of grief
veiling every page from first to last. Subtlety and variety are
falsified by such absoluteness.

The naming of Charles Swann

Introducing Swann as he is known to the family at Combray,
the narrator makes it plain, by the poetic analogy of the
circumstances in which Swann often appears in their midst

after dinner, that this 'knowledge' relies on very limited information. Hearing the bell tinkle as the garden gate opens, the grandfather will ask who can be coming in; a moment later Swann is recognised — his 'identity' with the person they know as Swann established beyond doubt — by the sound of his voice, usually speaking to the grandmother, who likes to roam about in the twilight. The as yet shadowy figure who comes into view is at once 'filled in' for the assembled family with the characteristics of their old friend and neighbour, whose parents were on intimate terms with Marcel's grandfather, and who hardly ever calls without bringing fruit from his garden, or perhaps the herbs needed in a recipe the great-aunt has asked him for. Thus at the beginning of this passage the instructions for 'sauce gribiche' have been mentioned as a typical request, and at the end of it, two pages later, Swann is remembered as 'scented with the fragrance of . . . a sprig of tarragon' (one of the ingredients of that sauce). In this manner Swann has been 'named', and has answered in every particular to his name.

At this very same period of easy intimacy, however, when for Marcel's family Swann's features seem the incarnation of all those evenings 'half-remembered, half-forgotten', mingled with some details connected with his parents, a large circle of friends in Paris associate Swann's name and his appearance with ideas of rarefied worldly elegance because they know he is on social terms with the Prince of Wales and the exiled pretenders to the French throne (the 'letter from Twickenham', p. 5 above), as well as with others of lesser rank but more exalted lineage. Two completely different sets of notions are thus firmly attached, by different people, to the same name; the same lanky physique, high forehead and beaky nose, and this observation is generalised by the narrator in the celebrated comment that no person is a material entity which can be consulted like a document; our social personality is the creation of other people's ideas. To move, in his memory, the narrator adds, from the Swann of whom he later gained 'a very precise knowledge', in order to go back to Swann as the family knew him in Combray, is therefore 'like leaving one person behind to go towards another'. The presentation of figures in the whole novel is governed by the principle that, in the matter of human personality, only partial truths are available to us; it seems, in fact, out of keeping with this principle that the narrator should claim to have known Swann later 'avec exactitude'. As we have already recognised, Swann is the exception to many of the novel's own rules, and it is not only because he can be studied in many different contemporaneous contexts that he presents a privileged case in this respect. Knowledge of him exists over a longer period, as well as more intensively within a particular one (that of *Un Amour de Swann*) than our knowledge, and the narrator's, of any other character but Françoise; and we are enabled to put together in a kind of mosaic the impressions Swann makes at various times and in many different situations. Despite all pleas for the suspension of judgment, all revaluations, revelations and caveats, we do arrive at something resembling a precise knowledge of Swann through the narrator's experience of him.

It is Swann's marriage which removes him from the world of Marcel's grandparents during the Combray period, in a gradual but final way, and constitutes the shadowy area in which all his doings become the subject of hearsay even for his former intimates. It is the same influence, with the mystery that arises from incomplete information, which surrounds Swann with glamour for the boy. As soon as he sees and falls in love with Gilberte Swann, Marcel feels an irresistible temptation to speak and hear at least her surname, and develops stratagems to satisfy his longing by leading conversations in the desired direction. Italicized in the text to suggest the intensity of this satisfaction, the name of Swann when pronounced by his father in answer to his questions causes Marcel to hold his breath,

for this name, superimposed on the place in me where it was always inscribed, weighed on me . . . seeming . . . fuller than any other name, because it was heavy with all the times when I had mentally uttered it in advance.

The seduction that Swann's name exercises on Marcel is

reproduced every time he hears it; and he feels it is impossible that his parents should not receive the same impression − 'it seemed to me they must be countenancing and sharing in my dreams, *and I was miserable, as if I had triumphed over them and depraved them*' (italics mine).

This dark extension of the power of imaginative pleasure appears strange in connection with the familiar phenomenon first described. Most readers will recognise the need to name the beloved or to speak of what is associated with that name; thus in *Un Amour de Swann* Swann himself drags the explorer La Pérouse into conversations, and eats at a restaurant called after him, because Odette lives in the Rue La Pérouse. This compulsion may well result in embarrassment; hardly in a sense of guilt. But we find in *Jean Santeuil* (in a section headed '*Evolution des idées bourgeoises*') an occurrence of the same idea of transferred guilt more openly formulated. Jean, as his mother ages, is aware that her standards of moral judgment have been relaxed through his contacts in the world outside his home; the narrator comments that she has learned to love all her son's faults one by one:

Love is our great initiator, our great corrupter . . . She had come to resemble her son.

Guilt incurred by the child, even when undiscovered, has for Jean as for Marcel the capacity to overflow the bounds of consciousness and the limits of silence, so that it infects the serenity of domestic life. We can link this unlooked-for effect of the name of Swann with what we shall learn of Mlle Vinteuil's instinctive beliefs about pleasure; biographical considerations must also be acknowledged as the probable source of such insights as this.

The rainbow of snobbery

An apprenticeship in self-knowledge is bound to include a study of the social world. The 'voice of experience' which glosses the child's view is often, in *Combray*, the voice of an adult in the fictional family rather than that of the mature narrator, but the piercing accuracy of physical vision in social encounters which precede such 'readings' is the child's.

His observation is dovetailed with his elders' alertness in the matter of Legrandin, an engineer from Paris who has a property in Combray, and is esteemed by Marcel's family for his beautiful manners and delicate sensibility. They do not know until later that Legrandin dabbles in literature, but the grandmother criticises a bookish preciosity in his conversation, of which we are given some delightful samples; it is a fluent pastiche of Romantic world-weariness and nostalgia for Nature. The short jacket and flowing tie Legrandin wears are signals the grandmother welcomes as reinforcing his claim to despise worldliness and above all snobbery, though she notices exaggeration in his habit of railing against the very existence of the aristocracy, especially as his sister has married a Marquis, who has an estate near Balbec in Normandy.

The unmasking of Legrandin as a paragon of snobs forms a gradually unfolding story over some eighty pages of *Combray*, always interspersed with the developing themes of Marcel's life and inner consciousness. The lightness and exuberance of Legrandin's moral portrait derive from its being put together by Marcel and his parents. Coming out of church one Sunday with his father, Marcel sees Legrandin ecstatically dancing attendance on a local landowner's wife, and when they meet him face to face he manages to omit any greeting apart from the animated twinkling of one eye, or rather a corner of that eye. After initial incredulity, Marcel's father becomes convinced that he is not good enough to be acknowledged by Legrandin in the lady's presence. This discovery is followed by the working out of an ingenious system for entrapping the engineer into fresh self-revelations, which afford both Marcel's parents great delight. The last match in this sophisticated game is played when, unknown to Legrandin, plans have been made to send Marcel and his grandmother on a seaside holiday, and the resort of Balbec has been fixed upon. During a casual conversation Legrandin happens to launch into a prose-poem about this very place, and after listening politely Marcel's father is able to ask whether he has friends in that region.

To avoid the necessity of promising 'to these bourgeois, these sons of solicitors or stockbrokers' an introduction to his sister the Marchioness, Legrandin replies wildly —

'J'ai des amis partout où il y a des troupes d'arbres blessés, mais non vaincus, qui se sont rapprochés pour implorer ensemble avec une obstination pathétique un ciel inclément qui n'a pas pitié d'eux.'

'Ce n'est pas cela que je voulais dire' interrompit mon père, aussi obstiné que les arbres et aussi impitoyable que le ciel. 'Je demandais pour le cas où il arriverait n'importe quoi à ma belle-mère et où elle aurait besoin de ne pas se sentir là-bas en pays perdu.' (p. 131)

'I have friends wherever there are groups of trees which have been wounded but not overthrown, clustering together to implore with pathetic obstinacy an inclement sky which has no pity on them.'

'That is not what I meant' interrupted my father, as obstinate as the trees and as pitiless as the sky. 'I was asking in case anything should happen to my mother-in-law, so that she might not feel alone there at the back of beyond.'

Legrandin has by now recovered his poise after his first frantic feint. He improvises a 'machiavellian' discourse on the character of the Normandy coast, winding up with the warning that the whole area is unsuitable for young persons of a sensitive or melancholy disposition, and retreating while still in full spate; but the truly machiavellian manoeuvre by Marcel's father has been gloriously successful.

There is in Legrandin's vice something so repellent to modern sensibility that we readily concur with him when he says it must be the unforgivable sin. In the nineteenth century, writers were often censured for the depiction of depravity, squalor, blasphemy and cruelty — themes now accepted as part of truth-telling and of moral purpose. It would be thought excessively naïve to reproach the writer with the faults of characters in his fiction, and our age has become, in an admirable sense, curious, tolerant and understanding; the defects of these qualities are moral uncertainty and helplessness. Our judgment has been refined, and simultaneously undermined, by the influence of informed literary criticism.

Snobbery presents a special problem for our forbearance. In the figure of Legrandin we have a study of it to put beside those of Fanny Burney, Mrs Gaskell, George Eliot, Jane Austen and Henry James, which generally give uncomplicated delight. But Proust's account of snobbery is not confined to delicate caricature, nor inspired by rage. In various guises it spans every aspect of social and emotional relations in the world his narrator inhabits, merging at one end of its spectrum with the bookish child's passive recognition of glamour in living persons, like the Guermantes, whose family names appear in history lessons, and at the other with activities such as the 'cutting' and 'dropping' of former friends. Those visitors who have ceased to be welcome at Aunt Léonie's bedside because their view of her condition has been either too sanguine or too gloomy, and who have to be turned away at the door, provide Françoise with the conviction that her mistress is superior to them since she refuses to see them; and thus Françoise too enjoys one of the satisfactions snobbery can bring. Swann does not expect Marcel's family to receive his wife, who has formerly been kept by other men besides himself. This, the inescapable convention of the time, results in the boy's attributing mysterious social superiority to Swann's wife, Odette, and to their daughter Gilberte, and he regrets that his mother does not use lipstick or dye her hair, as he has heard Mme Swann does. When to the prestige of inaccessibility is added the information, from Swann, that Gilberte is on easy terms with Marcel's favourite living writer, Bergotte, and that she goes with the great man to visit cathedrals and old towns, the accumulated magic reflected upon Marcel's mental image of the girl has become an emotional predisposition: 'it amounted to being on the point of falling in love with her.'

An essential element in this state of mind, and in the wide arc of snobbery, is the subjective consciousness of inferiority – 'then I understood both the value of a being such as Mlle Swann, and also how crude and ignorant I should appear in her eyes.'

Repeatedly, this sense of being excluded from a desired

intimacy by the irredeemable unworthiness of the perceiving self becomes, in the novel, the source of an obsession. Thus, it seems, each one of us apprehends the self in the moment of apprehending others, or one other. A fluid, vulnerable, almost a flabby little personage hides behind our eyes. Distressingly lacking in definition, it perceives firmness of outline in the threatening or implacable other, and becomes self-critical. This essentially twentieth-century self-perception links Proust with writers such as Thomas Mann, who derive it in part from Nietzsche's theories of temperament and of power, and for whom it is a means of distinguishing types – the artist and the man of action, for instance. Proust in an unemphatic way makes a different claim: the lesson to be drawn from his presentation of human personality is that of resemblance rather than of differing types. Given the capacity for emotional dependence on others, all of us, according to Proust, share this self-awareness to some extent and at various times. In Sartre's autobiographical fiction *Les Mots* we hear a strikingly similar note, and with the help of his philosophical writings we may conclude that his view is close to that of Proust. When the young Jean-Paul is said to have felt himself to be 'nothing: an ineffable transparency', or to have resigned himself to 'l'écœurante fadeur de ma disponibilité' – 'the nauseating insipidity of my indeterminate condition' – a statement is being made of general import, even though the child in his own time was unable to imagine that others in his world could have similar sensations about themselves.

As a consequence of these predispositions, Marcel's first sight of Gilberte Swann, a beautiful child framed in the flowering hawthorns which border her parents' garden at Tansonville, at once brings him the conviction that her sidelong, half-smiling glance conveys insulting contempt. A bizarre feature of this meeting is that Gilberte makes 'an obscene gesture' which Marcel takes for intentional rudeness, but which, long afterwards, she explains was an invitation, a compliment to his attractiveness. Feeling himself to be ridiculous to Gilberte, Marcel is hopelessly subjugated.

At that moment her name, called in a sharp voice by her mother from a distance, confirms that it is really Swann's daughter he sees: the name, like a talisman which will enable him to find her again, passes by Marcel, 'colouring like the rainbow all the zone of pure air it had traversed . . . with the mystery of her life' — a region he was not, he believed, to enter.

The 'rainbow' is the metonymic correlative to the 'vertical, prismatic fan' of water-drops already described as part of the vision of Gilberte, for she is standing near a garden hose which is spraying the flowers.

Mystery and unattainability arouse in us, then, mingled desire and subservience, the predisposition for love, or if not love then for an obsessive preoccupation which much resembles it:

Legrandin's snobbery never urged him to pay frequent visits to a duchess [because she was a duchess. Instead] it imposed on his imagination the task of making this duchess appear to be adorned with all the graces. Legrandin . . . congratulated himself on yielding to the charm of intelligence and virtue which horrid snobs are incapable of recognising.

To put this in perspective, we are told that Swann is not a snob; but he is a womaniser, or has been one in the period before the narrator's birth. To make a perfect equation of the contrasts between Swann and Legrandin, one term is missing. Legrandin, as it will ultimately turn out, is indifferent to women sexually; else we would find him sacrificing love to his snobbery. Of Swann the obverse is true. He treats his aristocratic friends as pawns in his pursuit of women who may be their wives or their obscure young relatives, or else their servants, on whom he can make an impression by name-dropping: 'And Swann, unaffected and casual with a duchess, was terrified of being underrated when he was with a housemaid, and was apt to start showing off.'

That we instinctively recognise superiority in those who attract us; that the idea of superiority in others, manifest in the power they wield over us, inevitably results in our finding them ever more attractive — this is the theorem which allows Proust to incorporate snobbery in his study of our whole experience of other human beings, including even the experience of passion.

The two themes, love and power, merge in the delineation of behaviour obeying the same laws under the influence of either.

Proust has often been reproached with being a snob. André Gide, who read, or glanced at, the manuscript of *Swann's Way* for a publisher in 1912, advised rejection because he found it 'too full of duchesses', and we may sympathise with him; with few exceptions, the duchesses in the novel are 'not real people' – as Marcel himself says in a different context. The word 'duchess' is a cipher, a kind of dead metaphor, and is not peculiar in this respect to Proust's usage; it is part of the heritage of Balzac of which he did not rid himself. But the apparent naïveté here is less crass than it may have seemed before the publication of *Jean Santeuil*. In that work, the vignette of a character called Desroches contains a digression on the snobbery of writers, based on Balzac's hero Lucien de Rubempré, a poet and would-be novelist in *Illusions perdues*. Proust sees the motivation of Lucien's social climbing not in the desire to be as rich and powerful as an aristocrat, but in the determination to share to the full the life he wants to use as his copy: '(an argument that, however, does not impel him to acquaint himself with poverty and mediocrity, which are forms of life as much as opulence is)', though it must be said that this judgment has lost sight of Lucien, whose early life has thoroughly acquainted him with poverty. The argument goes on, in *Jean Santeuil*, that 'the special psychological flora' of fashionable society includes snobbery as its most poisonous flower. The Proustian alternative 'soit que . . . soit que . . .' only to be clumsily rendered in English as 'whether because . . . or whether . . .' then offers us its urbane invitation to take part in the creative process –

And whether it is because he shrewdly takes pleasure in castigating in others the shame of these morbid symptoms he recognises in himself, or because to speak of his malady, even for the purpose of scourging it, is still a way of feeding and cherishing it, the novelist who is also a snob will become the novelist of snobs.

The magnetism of social status we call snobbery, and the

magnetism of the person we call love, are then shown as closely akin, and the passage ends with the maxim 'for desire, in snobbery as in love, is the origin and not the effect of admiration'.

The writing in *Jean Santeuil*, which was never finished or revised, is so unpolished as to give an almost physical impression of unevenness, yet the corresponding quality of an unwary experimental candour is likely to be precious to the reader who is disinclined to regard the text of *La Recherche* as sacrosanct. Stumbling from a phrase that seems shallow to one that opens fathoms deep, we are helped by *Jean Santeuil* to glimpse self-parody in the figure of Legrandin, with his post-Romantic flowers of speech and his attachment to Nature, and to duchesses.

Moral refinements and moral judgments

Somewhere along its prismatic arc, snobbery attaches itself to sanctimoniousness and enables the self-righteous to enjoy the worldly satisfactions of snubbing and 'cutting' which they would otherwise have to deny themselves. The moral issues which ordinarily seem clear − the baseness of fawning, the meanness of condescension − become troubled and full of hidden traps. M. Vinteuil, who has prudishly avoided greeting Swann since he married the disreputable Odette, later finds himself in an even more scandalous domestic situation, and is pathetically grateful when Swann speaks kindly to him of the daughter who is disgracing him. The narrator's family, generally presented in an ideal light, remain attached to Swann for the sake of their memories of his parents, and it is Swann who is grateful when Marcel's mother gently asks after the little Gilberte. But Swann is a problematic figure, always hovering on some invisible border-line (in 'a twilight zone, a *terra incognita*' as we read in *A l'Ombre des jeunes filles en fleurs*, p. 518), and he succeeds in confronting even their dignified loyalty with insoluble questions. The mention of his name in gossip columns, not only as a distinguished art-collector, but also as the guest and friend of the exalted, causes incredulity and then unease. Though the grand-mother's generosity of mind allows her to report without comment what she learns from Mme de Villeparisis about Swann's intimacy with the heirs of the Guermantes, Marcel's cross-grained great-aunt is not expressing her own view alone when she interprets that intimacy as proof of social climbing and forgetfulness of inherited obligations.

It is Swann's fate to incur rather similar resentments arising from quite another set of social judgments — more adventitious and far more self-interested than the great-aunt's provincial disapproval. In *Un Amour de Swann*, long before Marcel's birth, Swann arouses a passion of hostility in Mme Verdurin by failing to conceal entirely that he still visits other salons, and that some of them are very grand compared with hers. Since he has come to be dependent on her invitations for the meetings with Odette which form the chief interest of his life, Mme Verdurin can punish him for his intimacy with the great by excluding him from the 'little clan' she rules over. The penalty for Swann's aura of glamour, found so suspect in Combray, has thus formerly been exacted by Mme Verdurin with a vindictive relish which links it with Marcel's early discoveries of cruelty. One of these discoveries centres on Françoise, the other on the house called Montjouvain.

Moral evaluations are not outside the scope of Proust's novel; it would not otherwise have seemed to him to merit the name. But they are nearly always presented with the possibility of a revaluation, sometimes occuring hundreds of pages later. Often readers seem to be invited to draw moral conclusions, but in this respect as in others they learn caution as their reading goes on. Where the narrator offers his own deductions or judgments, they are taken into the pattern of learning which, as we have said, forms a link between this novel and the *Bildungsroman*, the story of an initiation into and education for life. In these judgements we are most likely to catch the note of tentativeness and of impending revision, which tells us how far Proust has travelled from the aims of realistic fiction. At the same time it recalls the French writer most firmly identified with realism in much critical thinking

– Honoré de Balzac, who likes to warn his readers against hasty responses, whether to the actions of his characters or to the literary techniques by which he represents them. Proust's tentativeness is often explicit in the musing 'peut-être', and the offer of alternative motivations with that 'soit que . . . soit que . . .' we have already seen.

Freedom of narrative procedure characterises the commentary or *discours* on what has been observed or reported; omniscience sometimes supersedes and conflicts with the tentativeness we have spoken of. This fluidity closely corresponds to the freedom of movement in time and space which the narrator makes use of most strikingly in the first and last sections of *Swann's Way* – a fluidity and freedom which contribute to the difficulty this part of the novel presents. Still, the mind which proceeds by intuitive leaps, and deductions from observation, to conclusions that are never irrevocable certainties, and which has always, as the shifting backdrops of its inner vision, scenes from the distant past, as well as objects, tasks, affections and fears that belong to the transient present moment – this mind is after all very familiar to us, because it is our own. Our own in all these respects, that is, but with the additional power of self-analysis few of us possess. Charles Swann is characterised by his reluctance to pursue any difficult train of thought; the narrator, as we have seen, accuses himself of mental indolence; yet we, the readers, quickly come to recognise this characteristic in ourselves, and to value the willed attention through which this writing illuminates our dim and fitful self-awareness. The portrait is turned into a looking-glass.

The study of Françoise, housekeeper to Aunt Léonie and later to Marcel's parents in Paris, forms a strand that runs from beginning to end of *La Recherche*. Proust's study of her shows the subtlest work of the moral imagination, not only in the portrait of Françoise herself, but also by setting her sensibility beside that of the narrator in their daily intimate contacts and conflicts. Françoise can be devious, unkind, vengeful and suspicious. She also embodies ancient virtues of conduct, ancient graces of speech and manner; though those of speech are to prove not immune from the forces of time and change. She is at the centre of an incident in *Combray* which we may compare with two others to illustrate the process of the refinement or overturning of judgments. The scene reveals to Marcel that the selfless and untiring servant is capable of cruelty. Oblique light is shed on it by two very different sets of reflections: one on an aspect of reading that unexpectedly unites Françoise and Marcel, the other on the lesbian lovers at Montjouvain.

Visiting the kitchen to find out what's cooking, the child one day sees Françoise in the scullery killing a chicken in uncharacteristic haste. The chicken is hard to despatch, and she is shouting 'Sale bête!' (more like 'Horrible thing!' than 'Dirty beast!') as she slaughters it with a knife, and even, after its head is off, while she collects the blood in a dish (not for the purposes of black magic, but, no doubt, for the hors d'œuvre called 'sang de poulet'). Marcel is filled with tremulous horror and he thinks of asking his aunt to dismiss Françoise, but even in his indignation he wonders who could possibly replace her as the provider of such delicious treats as she will make of this same chicken. He soon understands that this 'cowardly calculation' has been arrived at long before by the adults, who have better evidence of their servant's hardheartedness than the chicken's death; this is as it were a demonstration suited to the child's grasp. Her attitude to the human race is less easily forgiven, for apart from her immediate family and that of her employers, she can feel compassion only at a remove; those about her are the objects of her jealousy and suspicion, but she often weeps over newspaper reports of accidents and misfortunes. She has fallen for 'the pathos of the police-court', which Ruskin warns against in an unforgettable passage of *Sesame and Lilies* as a modern alternative to practical charity.

This defect in Françoise becomes clear to Marcel immediately after the chicken episode, in her relations with the kitchenmaid, known as La Charité. This is because in the voluminous skirts she wears to conceal her advanced state of pregnancy the girl has reminded Swann of the figure of Charity in Giotto's series of the Vices and Virtues at Padua, reproductions of which he has given to Marcel (they are the same, incidentally, that provide the illustrations and the themes of Ruskin's *Fors Clavigera*). When she hastily kills the chicken, Françoise is without help in the house because La Charité has just given birth and is lying very ill. Called to her bedside at night by her cries, Marcel's mother summons Françoise, but she reacts crossly and tells them the sufferer is 'play-acting'. Sent to consult a medical reference-book for first-aid measures, Françoise fails to return, and the boy finds her reading the clinical description of post-natal colic and in floods of tears over the case-history. Once at the bedside, she recovers her equilibrium and her bad temper, and assails the patient with 'frightful sarcasms' about the behaviour that has brought her to this pass. Years later, it becomes clear that even the splendid asparagus dishes which have been served almost every day in this season have been selected by Françoise with malicious intent, because cleaning asparagus gave La Charité such violent attacks of asthma that she was forced at last to leave the job.

The underlying causes of this cruelty are possessiveness and jealousy, and Françoise has driven away other assistants by other means to avoid sharing her employers' appreciation with them. Hers is a compound but not a complex nature, and there is a kind of comedy in this portrait that is not always separable from that of the traditional flat presentation of servants in earlier plays and novels. And yet in a great many episodes the narrator shows his own behaviour as crass in comparison with the delicacy of which Françoise is capable, and this is especially marked in their dialogues after the death of Léonie, whom she alone mourns 'with savage grief'. An extended validation, in which her name occurs only parenthetically, of the peculiar response Françoise has to the feelings of others, is implied in the course of the much-interrupted discussion of the boy's reading during the early pages of *Combray*.

Reading, in his childhood, is accompanied by the overlapping of simultaneous states of mind, forming a prismatic screen. The elements that compose the screen are listed, and range from the 'deepest hidden aspirations' of his nature to the simple exterior vision of the garden in which he is sitting. At the deepest level of consciousness, dynamically busy with the search for truth, is his belief in the philosophical wealth and beauty of the book before him. This belief is then attributed to his reliance on the good opinion of the particular book expressed by 'the teacher, or the school-friend, who appeared to me at that moment to hold the secret of truth and beauty, half-apprehended and half-incomprehensible, to attain which was the vague but unvarying aim of my thoughts'. Thus the inherent truth of literature is the object of belief, and the belief is at once exposed as unsound and faultily based, entirely contingent on the opinion of an acquaintance. Yet the value of such a manner of reading is not denied, is indeed reasserted by the reading child's blissful and whole-hearted absorption. It is a microcosm of the way Proust deals with the world. Beauty and truth are recognised in the world and grasped in the fiction, then undermined and relativised by the effects of time and the intellectual perception of the delusiveness of experience; at the conclusion of the process the original recognition is restored and reinstated with a new validity. Error and transience have been accepted and incorporated into our understanding.

In the same way the error Françoise commits by her failure to feel for those near her is obliquely referred to, and taken into a larger truthfulness, by the next element in the 'many-coloured screen' of Marcel's consciousness as he reads. This is his eager response to plot and events in his book, though 'it is true that the characters affected by them were not "real", as Françoise would say'. (Her name is not mentioned elsewhere in this meditation.) Real persons, the narrator continues, now adopting her terminology without quotation marks, 'however deeply we may sympathise with them, are to a great extent perceived by our senses, that is they remain opaque to us, offer a dead weight that our sensibility is incapable of raising up'. Our emotions are affected by the joys and sorrows of a real person only when an *image* of their joy or sorrow is interposed, requiring the suppression of the real, and concentration on 'a small part of the total notion we have of that person' before we can be sympathetically moved on his or her behalf. The invention − the innovation − of the first novelist, the narrator continues (and, we want to add, much more so that of the first tragic dramatist) was the idea of replacing these 'parts' that are 'impenetrable' to our feelings by an equal quantity of immaterial parts − this refers of course to the elements of characterisation. There is here an example of an almost naïve semi-scientific mannerism of Proust's in the suggested division into parts and quantities, into the impermeable and the assimilable, of what is evidently an incorporeal tissue of the utmost delicacy. The transparent overlapping sections of that 'screen' of the reading child's consciousness have already made us aware of this habit of mind, by which abstractions derived from physical experience are transmuted back again into material terms. This system, as it deserves to be called, has indeed something child-like about it, though it is by no means confined to childish occasions; in certain passages the analysis thus conducted results in a maxim whose force is poetic. Sartre accuses Proust of an old-fashioned, associationist and mechanistic approach to psychology, and the above argument is an example of what he objected to; but Sartre underestimates its directness and originality, just as he overestimates the importance of being 'scientifically' up to date in theoretical terms as a qualification for the exploration of the self.

The meditation on the obtrusive 'reality' of persons is relevant to the work of the artist's imagination. 'The invention of the first novelist' is necessarily recommenced by every novelist. Proust's method of writing, if we try to follow its development through the many tentative or fragmentary pages that are the precursors of *La Recherche*, shows the resolute sacrifice and paring of encumbering elements of 'the real' to liberate 'essence'. 'La vie réelle', which the narrator seems to glimpse beyond the trees at Hudimesnil, is equivalent to 'la vérité' − not at all to that 'reality of persons' so dense with circumstances and qualities that we cannot make their joy or sorrow our own. It is in reading that we experience the range of emotions it would take us many years to know in forms diluted by the slowness and the distractions of life. The narrator ends his argument by comparing this slowness to the slow changes of the human heart – a source of grief we also know only in reading or in imagination, since these changes in ourselves are mercifully veiled from us by their gradualness.

This passage, in which an aesthetic doctrine merges with a theory of reception, and whose main points I have tried to paraphrase, is closely related to the response Françoise makes to human suffering. The newspaper report and the clinical account of symptoms represent her reading, and offer the required opportunity to see a victim isolated from the 'dead weight' of incongruous facts that would cause antipathy in contact with a real person – the antipathy Françoise feels when she is confronted with the kitchen-maid on her bed of pain.

A more radical example of a moral assessment at first unequivocally stated and then tentatively modified occurs in the two episodes in which Marcel is an eavesdropper at Montjouvain.

By comparing the writing here with that of *Jean Santeuil* we get a clearer idea of some implications of the change, via *Contre Sainte-Beuve*, from third- to first-person narration. In *Jean Santeuil* there are whole chapters in which, since Jean himself is not present to act as focus, an unlocated voice provides information and reflections, but as alternate sections give Jean's subjective comments, that voice seems an unwarranted ramification of Jean's own. The change to first-person narration bestows a freedom more important than that of omniscience, and vital for the presentation of time as non-linear, with the power to juxtapose different moments from the narrator's past without the burden of explanations. Unity is thus established in the single intimate viewpoint of 'the one who says I', but Proust's narrator is at times in the position of a story-teller, and hankers after a story-teller's conventional omniscience. Where it becomes essential, plausibility is pursued, if not always achieved, by the device of eavesdropping. Even Aunt Léonie, who has little she wants to conceal except the fact that she occasionally sleeps quite well, is thus overheard in monologue as Marcel hesitates outside her open door, exclaiming that she has had a horrible dream that her husband had returned to life and was insisting on her taking a daily walk.

It is from a little shrubbery on a hillock, close to the first-floor windows of Montjouvain, that Marcel witnesses two separate scenes not intended for his eyes; these occasions are separated by a span of years during which M. Vinteuil, whose house it is, has gone into a decline and then died, leaving his daughter to live with her older woman-friend. In the first scene Marcel sees the dissimulation of the artist's innocent longing for appreciation; in the second, it is the surrender to physical desire that is dissimulated. Both, framed by the window and provided with audible dialogue, could be described as play-acting. The second is indeed so described, and the hidden observer's role in it is not only that of a reporter. Something less than candid links him firmly with the two girls he is watching and is expressed in the pretext he offers for remaining where he is − if he moves away, he will be heard, and 'Mlle Vinteuil might have thought I had hidden myself there to spy on her'.

The girls in any case choose to imagine that they are watched from outside, but their true spectator is the photograph of Vinteuil, prominently placed by his daughter before her friend comes in, just as Vinteuil himself on the previous occasion had placed the sheets of his own music on view before his callers entered the room. 'I don't know who can have put it there' he had replied to their enquiries after drawing their attention to it by removing it again − longing to be persuaded to play it for them, too shy to give way to their polite encouragement. His daughter uses the same words of the photograph to ensure that her friend will not omit the abuse of Vinteuil which 'no doubt' (the watcher or the narrator interposes) has become part of their 'ritual profanation'.

This 'sans doute' rather concentrates our attention on the split personality of our informant; there seem to be three of him in the shrubbery, and the third, who is the novelist, has become impatient with the demands of his own device for achieving plausibility. Over the shoulders of the voyeuristic Marcel and his adult self (the narrator) this third voice begins to explain Mlle Vinteuil in a way not available to an onlooker:

Elle cherchait le plus loin qu'elle pouvait de sa vraie nature morale, à trouver le langage propre à la fille vicieuse qu'elle désirait d'être, mais les mots qu'elle pensait que celle-ci eût prononcés sincèrement lui paraissait faux dans sa bouche. (p. 161)

She was seeking, at the greatest distance possible from her true moral nature, for the idiom appropriate to the depraved creature she wished to be, but the words she thought that girl would have spoken sincerely seemed to her false on her own lips.

First-person narration is in danger of collapse, and a slight strain on it continues to be felt even after Mlle Vinteuil has made up her mind to close the shutters, and *discours* has resumed its control over *récit*.

For now, in a strikingly Balzacian auto-critique, the narrator expresses a doubt that may correspond to the reader's own, though it ostensibly relates to the exact degree of Mlle Vinteuil's sincerity – as in the above quotation – whereas the reader's reservations are likely to extend to the convincingness of the narrator's 'discours' itself. The critique concerns the melodramatic quality of the scene Marcel has witnessed:

c'est à la lumière de la rampe des théâtres du boulevard plutôt que sous la lampe d'une maison de campagne véritable qu'on peut voir une fille faire cracher une amie sur le portrait d'un père qui n'a vécu que pour elle. (p. 163)

it is in the glare of the footlights in some popular theatre, rather than beneath the lamp of a real house in the country, that we may see a daughter incite her friend to spit on the portrait of a father who has devoted his whole life to her.

and the sentence concludes –

et il n'y a guère que le sadisme qui donne un fondement dans la vie à l'esthétique du mélodrame. (p. 163)

sadism is about the only thing in [real] life that gives a basis for the genre of melodrama.

The narrator's justification for using the words 'sadism' and 'sadist' several times in the ensuing *discours* is that Vinteuil's decline and death are seen, in Combray, to have been brought about by the shame of his daughter's lesbianism. Dr Percepied, at one extreme of opinion, jokes coarsely on the subject. Marcel's mother, at the other, wonders how divine justice will 'reward' Vinteuil's selfless devotion. But the narrator, starting on his re-assessment, comments that Mlle Vinteuil's behaviour is itself the dissimulation of her innate goodness, its theatricality the disguise demanded by her unselfishness and timid wish to conform. Mlle Vinteuil adopts a mask to shield her not against the world but against her own moral instincts. Theatricality, the narrator supposes, or rather states, is characteristic of her whole experience of pleasure. At some stage before Marcel spies on her, she has assumed the passive ingenuous role, and her friend that of the cynical seducer. These roles enable them to overcome Mlle Vinteuil's temperamental attachment to innocence and gentleness, inherited, like her blue eyes, from her father's side of the family. Sensual pleasure seems to her a privilege for which she must do violence to her tender and conscientious inclinations – to obtain it she must feel herself to be evil. The wicked sneers about her dead father and even an assumed viciousness of facial expression are designed as an indispensable arousal by the elder girl, to persuade Mlle Vinteuil of their shared degradation. Thus the narrator's conclusion, after re-examining Mlle Vinteuil's conduct in the light of his other knowledge, is that her fundamental goodness actually predisposes her to appear more vicious than she really is.

In his novel *The Man Without Qualities*, Proust's contemporary Robert Musil offers a somewhat similar insight into his character Bonadea; she often gives way to sexual caprice, but retains her inner equilibrium by the pretence that these episodes are a form of theatre –

What you see before you are stage-eyes, a stage moustache, the buttons that are being undone are part of a theatrical costume.

and thus wilfully suspends the normal conditions of the life she leads as a high-principled wife and mother.

The notion of evil, Proust's narrator argues, would have lost its exotic appeal for Mlle Vinteuil had she been able to recognise that our indifference to the suffering we inflict on others − 'the terrible and permanent form of cruelty' − is a common fault, not a rare and extraordinary condition. The duality of her nature is physiologically predetermined; when she first appears, at church with her father, she is a shy tomboy, sometimes taking fright at the gruffness of her own voice. In the scene witnessed through the window, this duality is more forcibly expressed in a metaphor drawing upon the external situation, when 'all the time, within herself, a timid suppliant virgin was imploring and warding off a rough overbearing warrior'. For all this complexity, and despite the melodramatic pathos of her father's dying of grief, she can, in the end, be likened to Françoise and to the majority of human beings in the simple failure of her imaginative sympathy, a failure seen as all but inescapable. The narrator's comments have after all successfully trodden a razor's edge of speculation − the characteristic 'peut-être' occurs six times in this one paragraph of evaluation and revaluation.

Later in the novel M. Vinteuil's 'reward' will be found to have emerged from the same set of circumstances that cut short his life. His music, infinitely precious to Swann and to Marcel, becomes widely known after being collated and transcribed by his daughter and her woman friend.

In contrast to Mlle Vinteuil and Françoise, whose acts of cruelty are first condemned by the narrator and then re-assessed with a refined understanding, *Un Amour de Swann* introduces, in Mme Verdurin, the portrait of a hypocritical bully, a monster for whom no relative moral considerations can induce our sympathy.

In the last paragraphs of *Combray* we are prepared for the opening of *Un Amour de Swann* with the words −

Thus until morning I would go on thinking of the Combray time
. . . and . . . of what I had learned, many years after leaving the little
town, of a love-affair Swann had had before my birth, with that
precision of detail which is sometimes easier to obtain concerning the
lives of people who have been dead for centuries than it is for [the
lives of] our best friends, and which [precision] seems impossible,
as it used to seem impossible to carry on a conversation from one
town to another – as long as we do not know of the device by which
[this] has been overcome.

This odd coded reference to the invention of the telephone is
perhaps perfunctory as an explanation of the wealth of
recollected detail we shall be given about Swann and Odette.
A certain magic surrounds the narrator's plunge into Swann's
past, still more audacious than his diving into the depths of
his own oblivion. Intended, it seems, as another dash at the
notion of plausibility in omniscience, like the shrubbery at
Montjouvain and various glazed panels and keyholes in later
episodes, this gesture towards the new technology turns into
a flourish of the necromancer's wand, a reminder of his power
to scan at a glance 'the order of the years and the worlds'.

It soon becomes apparent that we are not to forget the first-
person mediator in spite of his being so firmly relegated to a date
still far in the future. He interposes here and there to remind
us of the relationship between Swann's love-affair and what
has gone before in our reading, though chronologically
speaking it is still to come. Thus, in the long phase of Swann's
enslavement through jealousy, we are explicitly instructed to
link Marcel with Swann through that suffering –

he would go to his bed in anxiety, as I was to do myself some years
later on the evenings when he came to dine at our house, at
Combray.

Thus, too, retrospective light is shed on the affectionate but
somewhat fragile bond between Swann and the household at
Combray, put under strain long before the marriage with
Odette eventually destroys that bond:

Many years later, when I began to be interested in Swann's character
because of the likeness . . . to my own, I often asked to be told again
how, when a letter came from him, my grandfather (who was not
yet my grandfather . . .), recognising his friend's handwriting on the

envelope, would exclaim 'Look out! Here's Swann after something or other!'

The 'something' was always of the same kind — what Swann wanted was their help in the furtherance of a new love-affair by means of an introduction or an invitation, so that the grandparents-to-be were enlisted in the respectable or distinguished 'phalanx' of those 'whom Swann so cynically forced to serve as his pimps'.

To this phalanx Mme Verdurin is recruited when Swann seeks an introduction to her salon because he knows Odette is often there, and because he has been led to exaggerate the difficulty of meeting her elsewhere. Mme Verdurin's ascendancy over her guests, her 'band of faithful', is based on her inherited wealth, but more essentially on a kind of *arriviste* Bohemianism. All her little 'clan' must acknowledge her supreme sensitivity in artistic matters, or be cast out. The pianist 'Ski' the painter, 'Monsieur Biche', and young Doctor Cottard, her favourites when Swann meets her, are all, as belonging to her, to be considered at least potentially superior to other members of their professions. Above all, Mme Verdurin imposes a complete ban on frequenting other salons, and vilifies aristocratic hostesses for fear of their rival attractions.

Swann's critical faculty deserts him under the spell of his love for Odette, and he persuades himself that the Verdurins are the most sincere and most sensitive people he has ever known: 'how much more intelligent and more artistic then fashionable society!' he exclaims to himself. To his own 'fashionable' friends he expresses himself even more emphatically 'with a solemnity that was a new thing in him' — a tone which betrays itself before the narrator's comment warns us of his self-delusion:

'. . . I have reached an age at which one must make a choice, decide once for all whom to love and whom to disdain . . . Well!' he would add with the . . . emotion we feel when . . . we say a thing not because it is true, but because we enjoy saying it, and listen to it . . . in our own voices as if it came from outside ourselves, 'the die is cast, I have chosen to love only those who are high-minded, and to live from now on only in their company'.

Gradually discovering that Swann is much sought-after in the proud and exclusive society that is beyond her reach, Mme Verdurin, who has for months past urged on his love-affair, suddenly expels him from grace, and, still in Swann's presence, sets about arranging a new coupling for Odette — 'I have just room for you here [in the carriage] next to M. de Forcheville' she calls commandingly, when Swann is expecting to see Odette home as usual. At the same time Mme Verdurin makes a daring leap into a posture of moral disapprobation of Swann's overt dependence on her for his meetings with Odette; it is not the first time Swann's 'phalanx of pimps' has betrayed his interests. The instinctive, idyllically shared hypocrisy that forms the communion of the Verdurin marriage ensures her husband's support; gloating over Swann's 'stricken look' as he was left to go home alone, she exclaims to M. Verdurin —

Non, mais voyez-vous, cette sale bête!

Really, I ask you! disgusting beast that he is!

making unconscious use, the narrator points out,

like Françoise at Combray when the chicken was hard to kill, of the words that are drawn by the last throes of an inoffensive animal . . . from the peasant who is crushing the life out of it.

With this 'memory' of the mirroring incident from a time to come, the narrator announces his vigilant ubiquity, manipulates a new fold in the fabric of time, and achieves a new link of resemblance between varieties of cruelty.

Time and tense

The complex manipulation of time is part of Proust's project of fathoming the deep levels of our consciousness; original discoveries concerning our inmost awareness of time occur in almost every part of *La Recherche*. But in this respect *Combray* has a special place in the larger scheme; here, and in *Noms de pays: le nom*, attention is constantly focused on the different ways in which time passes.

Two questions — what happens *in* our memory — the mental faculty — and *to* our memories — 'nos souvenirs' — can be said to form the principal theme of the early part of *Combray* — the 'three openings'. The answers and illustrations elicited by these questions are then the guiding subject of the greater part of *Combray*. Chronological progression of a kind is observed, but childhood in these pages is a continuum; the perpetual interchange between incident, response, foreshadowing and reminiscence goes on independently of precise dating, and the exact age of the child at a particular moment is immaterial. In two difficult passages the narrator's own chronology contains contradictions, but the difficulties are illuminating in themselves. Generally, the adult narrator's speculative attitude to his past also extends to reminders of the gulf separating him in his present time of writing from his younger self, often sounding a brief note of wonder or regret. Thus in the novel's daring project we are not to lose our awareness of the distant vantage-point from which involuntary memory is recreating Combray, even while we are immersed in the details of life in that time and place.

In that characteristically ordered and repetitive existence, the alternation of the single event with what is habitual is conveyed through the tenses of verbs, rather than through adverbial phrases such as 'the next day', 'two weeks later' or 'in the following year'. Phrases such as this in fact occur — 'in that same year' may be found several times as a loose link between episodes; or again we know that at Aunt Léonie's house lunch is served an hour early on Saturdays to allow Françoise to go to market afterwards; but relatively speaking this kind of information is conspicuous by its absence.

Events which would be given generous space in most realist writing are elided, appearing only in parenthesis and, typically, after rather than at the time of their occurrence, that is, only when their effects have to be woven into the tissue of the narrator's consciousness. A grand exception must be made, if we contemplate the whole novel, of Marcel's grandmother's illness and death, which are related with their attendant circumstances in consequential detail. But Aunt Léonie's death, much more typically, is revealed only in a five-word parenthesis, when its practical consequence for Marcel, now adolescent, is a last, autumnal, visit to Combray, and a new freedom to take walks, alone now, in the direction of Méséglise.

It is relevant to glance again at the article Proust wrote for the *Nouvelle revue française* of January 1921, entitled 'A propos du "style" de Flaubert', the occasion being an evaluation of Flaubert by the critic Thibaudet. Proust points out that Flaubert's 'strict hermetic continuity of style' depends in part on verb-forms conveying prolongation of states, duration of periods of time, and the passivity of persons (who suffer events rather than initiating them). With characteristically flexible perception Proust recognises that, for example, the notion of duration is not always achieved, as we might expect, by the use of the imperfect, but sometimes instead by the past definite as in 'il voyagea', 'il eut beaucoup d'aventures', 'il évita les hommes' – he travelled, he had many adventures, he shunned people – (all from the story 'St Julien l'Hospitalier' in *Trois contes*). James Joyce, as it happens, was struck by this usage in Flaubert's writing, but only to pounce on it as a fault in one instance – the first sentence of 'Un Cœur simple' (also in *Trois contes*) in which the past definite is used to cover a period of fifty years. But Joyce's judgment was at fault here. After a succession of such phrases, Proust goes on, the imperfect in Flaubert's usage can by contrast become the tense of a single action at a precise moment; moreover, in the 'subdued colouring' ('*demi-teinte*') of repeated imperfects, the present indicative seems a sudden flash of daylight. A number of other grammatical peculiarities are noted as 'part of a new vision'; and in an attempt to define, in Flaubert, the idiosyncratic atmosphere conjured up in the reader's consciousness, which for Proust is always the essential quality of a writer, he adds that the condition of a person who is moving house, and suffering the attendant disruption and 'unreal décor', occasions a mournfulness akin to that created by Flaubert's style. In their wit and subtlety these pages, though hurriedly written, show Proust's critical abilities at their liveliest, and they fully account for his claim to admire Flaubert without being able to love him. This is not admiration of syntactical mastery alone, and in his often-quoted praise of Flaubert's 'blank spaces', Proust refers to a way of dealing with time and its ironies. The 'blank' he selects occurs at the point in Flaubert's *L'Education sentimentale* where Frédéric sees his friend, the workman Dussardier, struck down in the street-rioting of 1848 by the sword of a dragoon; when the soldier turns, Frédéric recognises him as Sénécal, who had recently been the most implacably radical member of the same socialist group as Dussardier. Frédéric is left 'béant' — gaping, or thunderstruck, and this is the only approach to a comment which Flaubert permits himself; the chapter ends there. (It is an episode that might have appealed to Evelyn Waugh, and which he could have treated in a similar way, but we may imagine that he would have omitted one word — the adjectival participle. In quoting the sentence Proust uses an exclamation mark — 'et Frédéric, béant, reconnut Sénécal!' — but there is none in the original; this faulty recollection no doubt further illuminates the effect of Flaubert's rigorous suppressions — the exclamation mark exists in the reader's mind, but is disdained by the writer.)

Proust reads this 'blank' as an ellision of time, and speaks of 'decades' passed over, for in the next chapter Frédéric is some years older. It is also, as we see, the ellision of emotional response to a stroke of historical irony. In this essay Proust makes a plea for greater simplicity in reading — 'people nowadays read badly' he says, and goes on to complain of misunderstandings in the reception of *Swann's Way*. He cites Flaubert's economy as a treatment of time which he finds touching, and close to his own concerns. Although it was not his own aim, or within his power, to narrate with this crispness, Proust seems to follow Flaubert's practice, while adapting it, in the subtlety with which he liberates his sentences from flat explanatory clauses by precision in the use of the tenses.

As we are especially aware in reading *Mme Bovary*, movements, connections and information about the causes of events may be avoided by this means, and it is thus that long stretches of *Combray* are related in the imperfect tense, which contributes to our sense of sharing in the flow of experience, dateless as a tranquil childhood is dateless. Moreover, to balance Proust's observation about Flaubert's usage, there are occasions within this flow of the habitual when the reader's expectations of a different tense are baffled, and conversations on particular matters, despite their circumstantiality, are introduced in the imperfect. This happens in the dialogues between Françoise and Aunt Léonie, where the verbs of speech are in the imperfect, while the direct speech itself refers to the fleeting momentary details of what Léonie has seen from her window, or of the day's arrangements. The reader comes to accept the notion of recurrence imposed by forms such as 'soupirait ma tante' – 'my aunt would sigh' – 'répondait Françoise' – 'Françoise would reply' – although the events being discussed are not repeatable; Léonie wants to know, for instance, where Mme Imbert can have got the magnificent asparagus she was carrying home, or whether Mme Goupil, who seemed to be very late going to Mass, had arrived after the elevation of the Host. In essence, however, such incidents convey only minute variations within endless monotony. This monotony is so complete that on three separate occasions Léonie is alarmingly exercised by seeing or hearing of unfamiliar creatures (one of them a dog), for there are never any strangers in Combray; and indeed these three exceptions are rapidly disposed of when they are found to 'belong' to neighbouring families. Thus the quotations from Léonie's conversations are typical, not precise, and the tense used to introduce them corresponds to the inventive-anecdotal present in common daily speech. We might well say in English 'Then Françoise comes in and tells her'; or 'at this point someone asks an awkward question' and we also use, colloquially, a future tense, as in 'And then my aunt will insist' – 'she'll shake her head and say' which, while evoking the habitual, may very well introduce some newly invented particularity to highlight it.

Events which are not part of this habitual existence are

recounted in the past definite tense and sometimes given a date, or rather a place in time, relating them to the 'series' they belong to, and in which they mark a progression or an irreversible change. Such a change is brought about by the evening when Swann's coming to dinner, as he has often done before, causes Marcel's unprecedented emotional crisis. The discoveries about Legrandin move forward in successive scenes and, like the Montjouvain episodes and the wedding in the church of St Hilaire where Marcel first sees the Duchess of Guermantes, are also told in the past definite tense. The term 'series' seems appropriate because the definitive character of these incidents is qualified by their having been foreshadowed and, however briefly or allusively, anticipated. Certain places, persons and themes are as it were promised more than once before they move into full focus, so that for the reader as for Marcel they are in part familiar when the meeting, the revelation or the crisis concentrates attention on them.

Recurrence, in fact, is typical not only of the daily routine of Combray but also of episodes which, by contrast, arouse an intense response or become the matter of the narrator's long preoccupation. The second Montjouvain incident echoes the first; mysterious discrepancies in Legrandin's behaviour hint at his true weakness long before it is revealed, and the encounters with Gilberte and the Duchess are imaginatively summoned and heralded by Marcel's daydreaming; indeed the girl and the lady are part of the given world of Combray, pre-existent to any anecdote or speculation, the one as belonging to Swann's family and the other because her ancestors are represented in the stained-glass windows of St Hilaire. Foreknowledge and anticipation provide a mirror-image of memory, so that the life of this novel does not take shape in a sequence of events coming suddenly upon the protagonist, but is an ebb and flow of awareness, a varying alertness to possibilities. In this way time attains a self-reflecting quality; without recourse to notions of the occult, Proust's method allows him to suggest the dim outlines of the future just as constantly projected as the clear outlines of the

past. If 'the future' involves the idea of a place or a person,
these dim outlines have to be re-drawn when the real place or
person is first seen — it is a task that cannot be deferred, and
one demanding an effort of the will. Marcel's cherished mental image of the Duchess is confronted with her real presence
in church at the wedding of Dr Percepied's daughter, and the
effort to 'fit' (*appliquer*) the new image to the one that exists
in his mind is likened to the vain attempt to bring together
'two discs separated by a gap' — a simile of that arbitrary,
naïvely 'scientific' kind we have noted (p. 60 above). The real
Duchess is not (and could not be, as he now abruptly
recognises) a figure in a tapestry or in stained glass, and
Marcel is disappointed not because she is less beautiful than
he imagined but because, as a real woman, she resembles
others in his ordinary experience; she has escaped from the
infinite possibilities of the future.

In the encounter with Gilberte on the walk near her home
at Tansonville, Marcel is similarly confronted with the real
person emerging from his daydream, yet his impressions of
this incident are quite different. Perhaps, after all, Gilberte's
delightful appearance has some bearing on this difference.
But the true explanation is in the fidelity with which this
encounter reproduces the 'dim outlines' in which it has been
anticipated. The frame of flowering hawthorns in which
Marcel catches sight of Gilberte links her to an intense
experience of seeing and apprehending, entirely occupying his
attention at that moment as a resumption, a recurrence of a
process begun on an earlier occasion. This occasion is
separate from the glimpses of Gilberte in Marcel's mental
world which have arisen, for instance, from Swann's describing her as Bergotte's companion on sightseeing visits, or from
general notions of her mother's elegance and shady glamour.
It is, indeed, not an appearance of Gilberte but a premonition
of her, in which she is not named.

This premonitory may-blossom is used to decorate the altar
of St Hilaire at Saturday evening services intended for young
people and known as 'le mois de Marie' — the month of
Mary. This special Mass was one manifestation of the cult of

the Virgin which was widely propagated under the Emperor Napoleon III (from 1852 onward), and given new impetus after the French defeat of 1871; in Proust's own early childhood, religious revival was offered as an atonement for past sins to which the national disaster was attributed. Mariolatry with all its pretty fancies makes a strong contribution to the imagery of the two main passages about the hawthorn blossom in *Combray*. As perceived by Marcel, the presence of the living flowers in church suggests a union of the sacred with rustic simplicity. The hawthorn branches, running and intertwined as though growing on the altar, have been arranged by human hands, but 'Nature herself' has 'cut out' the shapes of the leaves, and added, 'as a supreme adornment', the clusters of dazzling white buds and flowers, profusely strewn 'as if on the train of a wedding dress'. We shall need to return, in speaking of imagery, to this apparition of Nature as *couturière*. Here our interest is rather in the culminating point of this first contemplation of may-blossom, where Marcel's delving after its essential quality permits him to see the open flowers as holding their bouquet of stamens 'si négligemment' — so casually — that 'following, trying to mime in [his] inner self' this 'gesture', he imagines it as 'a movement of the head, careless, rapid, with the coquettish glance, the narrowed pupils, of some blonde girl, scatterbrained and full of life'.

The borrowed sanctity of the hawthorn blossom has vanished, and Marcel's quest for essences is satisfied here, at least, with a very human resemblance — a preliminary sketch of Gilberte as she will appear to him at Tansonville.

Time out of joint

The way in which childhood time is presented in *Combray* tends to exclude divisions or make them seem superfluous. Yet decisive moments, recalled or anticipated, make their own dates and impose a 'before and after'. In at least two passages, events conflict with our sense of this decisiveness, and time seems to undergo a bewildering slip. These difficulties are distinct from some irreconcilable references to historically datable events, which defy enquiry. But it would not be candid to ignore striking anachronisms within this novel's own narrated time.

Two such puzzles, then, occur in the main part of *Combray*, one near the beginning of the 'recapturing' of memories of Léonie's house, the other towards the end, just after the meeting with Gilberte. The first, part of the account of Marcel's reading, but delaying its introduction, causes a shift in our vision of the child so that we are forced to see him as already adolescent; the second reverses the process, and where we have been lulled into supposing Marcel approaching adolescence, the circumstances show him to be a small child. If his age, explicitly stated or apparent, were the only source of discrepancy, we might resort to our belief that exactitude in this matter is always irrelevant in *Combray*, and that having, indeed, lulled us into the assumption that time is passing in this novel as it does in others, the writer is administering a calculated shock, and bringing our attention back to the multiple-layered transparency which allows different moments from the narrator's past to appear side by side.

But the temporal mystery in the first of our two incidents cannot be disposed of in this way. The discrepancy affects Marcel's very existence in the world at the relevant time, for the behaviour of the principal figure in the scene strongly suggests that it could only have taken place before his birth. This central figure is identified as a very pretty lady in a pink silk dress with a necklace of pearls, whom Marcel finds visiting his bachelor great-uncle Adolphe in Paris. So far, only ten pages have been devoted to the recaptured memory of Combray, and in a Balzacian digression beginning 'Voici pourquoi . . .' − 'This is why' − the narrator is explaining how a quarrel had occurred between Adolphe and the rest of the family. Marcel is out alone with his parents' permission to consult the theatre-announcements, and he knows it is a day of the week when Adolphe is not at home to his relatives. Admitted by the servant without being announced, Marcel instantly sizes up the lady as not only 'une cocotte' but 'une cocotte chic' ('an elegant adventuress', as we may put it) and is charmed by her cajoling subservient manner to his uncle, who, however, is embarrassed by the boy's arrival to the point of surliness with both his guests. What particularly vexes Adolphe is the lady's insisting that she knows both Marcel's parents by sight, sees a resemblance, finds him adorable, and so on; her behaviour is so winning from Marcel's point of view that he wonders how it is that a woman of this kind can resemble 'a girl of good family'; for as 'une cocotte chic' she must have some wealthy protector, and Marcel is unable to see what satisfaction the supposed millionaire would derive from squandering his money on the person before him. The unexpressed comparison in Marcel's expectation here is with an aloof imagined siren, both flashy and cruelly haughty; we may recall Mlle Vinteuil's instinctive notion that sexual pleasure, being evil, cannot co-exist with good-natured openness.

The boy who can form these judgments about his uncle's friend, but who is not yet allowed to go to the theatre, would appear to be in his early teens. When we later learn that the lady in pink was Odette, the chronological problem posed by this incident seems fairly flagrant. Since Gilberte Swann is the same age as Marcel, the lady he encounters at his uncle's has already been a mother for twelve or fourteen years, and her meekness in the face of Adolphe's insulting curtness, as well as her reference to the Grand Duke who is 'jealous' of him, seem strikingly inappropriate to the dignity of Mme Swann. After allowing for every kind of fluidity in the time-scheme of *Combray*, the reader is still left with the impression that Marcel has seen an eidolon or ghost of Odette representing an earlier stage of her life, when she might still seem to an observer 'like a girl of good family', and when she was in the habit of paying calls on men who treated her with little respect. There is no logical solution to this difficulty; but we may connect it with the description of Odette later in the novel as having the power of defying time, adopting new styles of beauty as fashions change, and appearing refreshed, as she ages, into a new seductiveness.

The second stumbling-block to our need for some chronological sequence is an episode giving an insight into the use of autobiographical notes of earlier date, rather sketchily retouched for *Combray*. It is the third and last of the 'series' dominated by the hawthorn flowers, and it occurs soon after the first meeting with Gilberte, linked with it by the words 'That same year'. In this short paragraph Marcel bids a tearful farewell to the hedge at Tansonville while it is still in bloom, because his family are leaving Combray at an earlier date than in other years. His unruly behaviour, as well as the circumstances, suggest infancy rather than the pre-adolescent stage in which we have been inclined to place his silent encounter with Gilberte. We know that even very young children can fall in love, especially at first sight, but it is harder to accommodate to infancy what we have been told of Marcel's longing to see Gilberte because she is a favourite of Bergotte, whose novels he admires.

On the morning of his enforced departure from Combray, got up in curl-papers and with a new hat and a velvet spencer for a visit to the photographer, Marcel runs away and is found by his mother on the Tansonville path with his finery in ruins, sobbing as he embraces the hawthorns. A few pages in the fragment *Retour à Guermantes*, appended with others to *Contre Sainte-Beuve* (and written in the first person like the rest of that work), are the recognisable origin of this scene, and describe an escapade of the narrator's little brother Robert at the age of five. It will be remembered that Proust's own brother Robert was two years his junior, and the episode is clearly a straightforward account of what must have become a treasured family anecdote; so straightforward, indeed, that it is far from lucid, for truth is not only stranger than fiction but as a rule much more complicated. Robert's farewell is not spoken to a flowering hedge but to a little pet goat he has been given during the holidays; he has just discovered this adored animal is not to accompany him home to Paris. The elder brother views Robert's anguish with detachment, seeing a fat-faced, sturdy child with torn lace petticoats and a mop of black corkscrew curls setting off his contorted features, ribbons dangling, his satin purse trampled.

As he is led back to the house, the rebel makes a spirited attempt to shame his mother by favourably comparing the goat's behaviour to him with her own.

These are the very sentiments Marcel addresses to the hawthorn hedge in *Combray*, though his language is slightly more elevated. Having changed the story of Robert and the goat to one of Marcel and his beloved blossom, Proust uses it as a brief comic rounding-off to the important and otherwise tenderly solemn 'hawthorn series' after its culmination in the appearance of Gilberte. Comic and final as it is, the farewell to the Tansonville hedgerow, placed earlier, would have jeopardised the intensity of that theme; yet the element of childishness still inherent in the reworked story undoubtably dislocates the narrator's own chronology.

We must suppose that Proust preserved this anecdote because he was fond of it, and the reason should be clear in both versions. A feature common to them is the parental vision of the scene as mock-heroic, a vision enjoyed by the elder brother looking on in the first version, but perforce merged in Marcel's 'memory' in *Combray*. Thus –

ma mère me trouva . . . comme une princesse de tragédie à qui pèseraient ces vains ornements, ingrat envers l'importune main qui en formant tous ces nœuds avait pris soin sur mon front d'assembler mes cheveux – foulant aux pieds . . . mon chapeau neuf.(p. 145)

my mother found me . . . like a tragedy queen oppressed by these vain adornments, ungrateful towards the over-zealous hand which twining all these curls had spared no pains to gather all my hair upon my brow – trampling my new hat underfoot.

This is a slightly paraphrased quotation from the complaint of Racine's Phèdre in her opening scene:

> Que ces vains ornements, que ces voiles me pèsent!
> Quelle importune main, en formant tous ces nœuds,
> A prissoin sur mon front d'assembler mes cheveux?

> O how these useless jewels, these veils oppress me!
> What over-zealous hand, entwining all these curls,
> Has laboured thus to pile my hair upon my brow?

and has been applied, verbatim except for the pronoun 'his'

for 'my', to Robert in the corresponding passage of the fragment in *Contre Sainte-Beuve*. Marcel's grandfather and his mother often resort to such games of classical allusion, and we seem to hear their voices perfecting and embroidering the recital of the episode. This literary game becomes the narrator's own, just like Swann's habit of assimilating people around him to figures in paintings by the Italian masters. Primarily parodistic, the game is capable of providing analogies for all occasions, including the solemn or the tragic. Thus on the surface of the Vivonne the long-stemmed water-lily straggling across the current, and perpetually passing from one bank to the other, reminds Marcel not only of the restless efforts of some neurasthenic, like Léonie, to escape self-induced and compulsive sufferings, but also of one of the tormented souls in the *Inferno*, whom Dante would have questioned —

if Virgil, striding ahead rapidly, had not forced him to follow at once, as my parents did me.

The episode of Marcel and the hawthorn blossom, formerly that of Robert and the goat, has a function separate from its anecdotal content. It is confusing on the chronological level, and on another level too — boisterous unruliness is nowhere else displayed by Marcel. But in the way it is absorbed through the comic literary parallel into family lore, the episode illustrates the means by which the past and the inner life of the novel's central figure become coherent to the reader. Such mental mannerisms as this of literary analogy-seeking, with their remote origins and models in our upbringing, exist in our innermost selves as cultural traces. Proust's narrator gives a kind of personal being to these traces. In *Sodom and Gomorrha* he reflects that his own individuality consists of a good many 'little interior persons'. Some of these, he imagines, will be gradually vanquished by time and illness. But he believes that one of the last to succumb will be 'a certain philosopher who is never happy but when he has discovered, between two works, between two sensations, a common element'. We are perhaps accustomed to suppose that such a habit of mind as this must be based on culture in the literary sense, and indeed this is the precondition for the examples we have just met with. But something very like the habit of this internal philosopher exists in a great variety of unliterary people too, those who comment on a happening with parallels drawn from experience or hearsay, those who grasp by such means the broad human significance of a single occasion. Certainly no cultural barrier could prevent most of us from recognising the other miniature self who is spoken of in the same part of *Sodom and Gomorrha* as likely to outlive all the rest of the narrator's hidden personalities, and whom he imagines as very much like the weather-manikin in the optician's window at Combray. This figure had a cape which he took off when the sun shone and put on when it was going to rain. Proust, in the guise of his narrator, says that if a shaft of sunlight should happen to fall across his own deathbed, this 'barometric little person' will certainly feel much better, and will sing out 'Aha! At last it's turned fine.'

The tendency to seek analogies is an aspect of that thinking in metaphors which is innate in all of us, and which in Proust was of course developed to the highest degree. Reading his novel, we come closer to understanding and valuing this faculty as much in ourselves as in the writing, and may remember the promise, or the hope, expressed in *Time Regained*, that the book would provide readers with the means of reading in themselves.

Imagery

In the lecture which concludes *The Use of Poetry and the Use of Criticism* (1933) T. S. Eliot formulates a Proustian idea more simply than Proust does, yet in suggestively similar terms. Eliot has said that only part of an author's imagery comes from his reading, and goes on:

It comes from the whole of his sensitive life since early childhood. Why, for all of us, out of all that we have heard, seen, felt, in a lifetime, do certain images recur, charged with emotion, rather than others? The song of one bird, the leap of one fish, at a particular time and place, the scent of one flower, an old woman on a German mountain path . . . such memories may have symbolic value, but of what we cannot tell, for they come to represent the depths of feeling into which we cannot peer. We might just as well ask why, when we try to recall visually some period in the past, we find in our memory just the few meagre arbitrarily chosen set of snapshots that we do find there, the faded poor souvenirs of passionate moments.

This last sentence, with its glance at a notion of voluntary memory and the perhaps defeatist association of it with the visual alone, is more striking than the rest of the quotation. The reason Proust's statements of such ideas are more complex is that he has greater faith in the possibility of 'peering into the depths of feeling' by the exploration of any sensory experience however apparently trivial. In his boyhood Marcel believed that, if he were ever to become a writer, he would have to start by identifying a great intellectual idea — 'some theme in which I would be able to express infinite philosophical meaning' (*Combray*, p. 173). In the event, theories were to reveal themselves not before, but during, the writing to which he would be impelled in what seemed to him a desultory way — by responding to the messages of his senses. Perceiving analogies, and using them metaphorically, was to be the way to mediate between the instinctive and the intellectual. The supremacy of imagery among the writer's instruments is most consistently asserted in *Le Temps retrouvé* (vol. III, p. 889). The narrator, waiting in the Guermantes library and following his new train of thought — or the author, as he now knows he is to be, hastily assembling his guiding principles before starting work — or the novelist, Proust himself, tacking on an explanation and a creed at the end of the book because it didn't fit in anywhere else — this composite informant remarks that the artist's pursuit of the truth depends upon his reproducing the multiplicity of sensations aroused by any 'image' we encounter in life; and continues:

What we call reality is a certain relation [rapport] between these sensations and the memories that simultaneously crowd in upon us — a relation that is obliterated by a simple cinematographic vision, which recedes all the further from the truth because of its claim to represent nothing else — a unique relation which the writer must discover in order to join its two terms together for ever in his phrase. One may, in a description, offer an interminable succession of the objects present in the place described, [but] the truth can only begin from the moment when the writer takes two different objects, establishes their relation, analogous in the world of art to the unique relation of the law of causality in the world of science, and encloses them in the necessary links [les anneaux — links of a chain] of a fine style; and similarly when, as life does, bringing together two sensations by the quality they share, he extracts their common essence by uniting them, to protect them from the hazards of time, in a metaphor.

No fine style here; but these words enable us to connect this contrast between a dreary photographic realism and the superior truthfulness of impression and sensation with what was said almost at the beginning of *Combray* about the relative truthfulness of voluntary and involuntary memory. The one is factual, cinematographic, 'meagre, arbitrarily chosen'; the other brings us, 'as life does', the totality of our physical and spiritual experience in harmonious coherence. The starting-point is in the physical world — the object, and then its reflection in the perceiving senses. Metaphor is the instrument by which these sensations make their smooth progress out from themselves, like widening circular ripples on water, to find their correlatives in memory and ideas. The smoothness and the harmony resemble the surface texture of paintings by the great masters — as Proust wrote in a letter to Mme de Noailles in 1904 (*Correspondence générale*, vol. II, p. 86). When the writer succeeds in carrying this process into effect, it constitutes an imitation of the action of involuntary memory confronting the present experience with a sensation from the past. Acknowledging this conception of metaphor as a means of conveying something of the individual inner life, on the very edge of what can be accomplished with words, we are better able to understand Proust's dictum in his article on Flaubert that —

La métaphore seule peut donner une sort d'éternité au style.

Metaphor alone can give a kind of eternity to a style.

For the ability to register resemblances and impose them as valid — without which this resource could not be deployed — is the key to the immense task of doing justice to the complexity of universal human experience, in which the dissolving and overlapping perceptions of a few seconds of time demand many hours and many words to record. This, at any rate, is the aim which presents itself to the narrator, and the word 'universal' is important. There is, for all the attentive effort required of the reader of *La Recherche*, no hint in it of the attitude T. S. Eliot shows to his potential public when he speaks of his idea of writing a verse-play in which —

> one character ['s] sensibility and intelligence should be on the plane of the most sensitive and intelligent members of the audience . . . the other personages . . . were to be material, literal-minded and visionless . . . there was to be an understanding between this protagonist and a small number of the audience, while the rest of the audience would share the responses of the other characters in the play.   (*The Use of Poetry*)

This project betrays a certain 'literal-mindedness' in an inappropriate quarter. It is of interest to us here only because it shows the impossibility of finding a parallel to it in the theories of Proust. Some of the personages of *La Recherche* are, indeed, 'material' and visionless, others ill-educated or intolerably pretentious. What we learn, if we will, from the novel, is the hard lesson that no person is all of a piece, that astonishment may always be in reserve for us in the behaviour and even in the capacities of people we think we know perfectly. The trained sensibility of Charles Swann lapses into boorishness under certain conditions; Françoise is the narrator's superior in delicacy of feeling and in altruism, though she is also ignorant and ruthless. How, then, to ensure that 'the rest of the audience' will conform to the role assigned to them for a sufficient span of time? No such expectation is expressed in Proust's anticipations of a future reading public.

Time, metaphor and St Hilaire

In the first distant view from the train (see above, p. 41), the town of Combray was 'nothing but a church'; St Hilaire, like

a grey-cloaked shepherdess, dominated and stood for all
the rest. The blocks and masses of the text which follow,
introducing themes and figures of the novel, are organised
about, and often return to, the architecture of the church as
well as the hours of reading which take place within sight of
it or within the sound of its bell. St Hilaire's architectural
presence acquires significance for the structure of the novel in
the image already quoted, in our summary of *La Recherche*
(see above, p. 22), in which the physical space occupied by the
church is expanded into a fourth dimension, invisible and yet
perceptible in its chapels, spread like wings across the centuries, in the thickness of its walls, the contour of its spire
against the sky, and in the 'Merovingian darkness' of its
crypt, so that St Hilaire seems to prevail over 'not a few
square yards, but successive epochs from which it emerged
victorious'.

The image of his novel as a cathedral, and an early notion
of giving its chapters architectural titles (Porch, Apsidal
Windows) are mentioned by Proust in a letter (to Count Jean
de Gaigneron, of August 1919). For him this image symbolis-
ed the solid interdependence and interlinking of the parts of
the whole structure, and in its origin appears closely related
to his narrator's vision of St Hilaire. The church has a
delicate pointed belfry and, beside it, a partly ruined square
tower of earlier date. From different parts of the town, the
spire seems to impose order on the streets and houses in views
which the narrator compares with his later mental 'épreuves
et gravures' − prints and engravings − of dominating spires
in other townscapes, only to find that, 'however tastefully'
his memory has 'executed' them, these other impressions lack
the quality conferred on St Hilaire by his having long believed
it to be unique. Thus the church serves to remind us of the
persistence of the world of Combray into his own present
time; for (as he tells us) he has often, in an unfamiliar quarter
of Paris, been brought to a standstill by the sight of a church-
spire which seems about to guide him at the next turning into
a street he knows; 'mais . . . c'est dans mon cœur . . .' −
'but . . . it is in my heart . . .' A rare form of punctuation in

Proust's prose, these dots seem to correspond here to the absentminded reverie to which, for once, no further verbalisation is appropriate.

But the measuring of time for the boy reading in the garden, of time wholly contained within a Combray Sunday afternoon, also belongs to St Hilaire as its bell rings out the hours:

Et à chaque heure il me semblait que c'était quelques instants seulement auparavant que la précédente avait sonné; la plus récente venait s'inscrire tout près de l'autre dans le ciel et je ne pouvais croire que soixante minutes eussent tenu dans ce petit arc bleu qui était compris entre leurs deux marques d'or. Quelquefois même cette heure prematurée sonnait deux coups de plus que la dernière . . . l'interêt de la lecture, magique comme un profond sommeil, avait donné le change à mes oreilles hallucinées et effacé la cloche d'or sur la surface azurée du silence.   (p. 87)

And when each hour struck it seemed to me that the previous one had chimed only a few moments earlier; the most recent came to inscribe itself close to the one before in the sky, and I could not believe that sixty minutes had been able to fit into the little blue arc contained between their two golden marks. Sometimes this premature hour even sounded two strokes more than the last . . . the interest of reading, as magical as a deep sleep, had deceived my hallucinated ears and blotted out the golden bell on the azure surface of the silence.

A characteristic aspect of the use of metaphor in Proust's writing becomes apparent in these two sentences. A mental impression is simply stated: absorbed in a book, the reader loses his normal awareness of an hour's duration. The sentence continues with the unexpected 'inscribing' of the hour on a celestial dial, or rather on a small arc of it, appearing as the chime is heard. The space for this arc between the chime now apprehended and the previous chime is smaller than seems appropriate, its diminutiveness suggests the rapidity with which time has passed, yet it also evokes the actual span between two figures on a clock-face. Five minutes are represented by that span; but if we think of the other hand of the clock, we understand the five minutes as an hour ('sixty minutes . . . fitted in'), and thus the simple act of reading a clock-face may itself stand for a metaphorical way of thinking. We can confirm that this notion is not fanciful by consulting a child of our own day, one whose ability to tell the time is limited to digital clocks and watches, and to whom a conventional clock-face conveys nothing − it is a metaphor in need of elucidation. The adjective 'analogue', applied to time-pieces, refers to the analogy, or the metaphor, of the sun's daily course, embodied in the traditional dial − which we have also learned to read as a doubling, referring it either to the hours of light or those of darkness. The tower of St Hilaire has no clock-face; it is on the blue sky that the little arc is imprinted, defined by two golden marks; aural reading of the hour becomes visible reading to the mind's eye. This kind of interchange between the messages of the different physical senses is the inexhaustible source of metaphor for Proust, and forms part of the kinship he acknowledges with Baudelaire. With the second sentence in the quotation we are returned to a not unfamiliar effect of absentmindedness. Three strokes resound, perhaps, when the boy who is reading recalls having heard the stroke of one, but not that of two o'clock. Again, the rest of the sentence reverts to the metaphor of the hour set against the sky, but now aural perception conveys the colours without the precise definition of vision, and the bell has become a golden sound on a blue silence. This is not the only occasion when the sound of the bell in its temporal function gives rise to a visual metaphor. On Sundays in fine weather, the members of the household sit down to lunch when they have just returned from Mass, and their dining-room is pervaded and invaded by physical reminders of the church that has been the focus of the morning hours. Even the bread on the table has been to church with them to be blessed. When at their meal they hear the midday chimes begin, the boy 'sees the time' as

l'heure altière de midi, descendue de la tour de St Hilaire qu'elle armoriait des douze fleurons momentanés de sa couronne sonore.
(p. 70.)

the haughty hour of midday, descending from the tower of St Hilaire which it emblazoned with the twelve momentary fleurets of its sonorous crown.

In their brief yet full development, these two metaphors exemplify not only the synaesthesia we have spoken of, but also the metonymic character by which Proust's metaphors are often distinguished. Metonymy is a figure of speech familiar in everyday usage and journalistic cliché, where a part is referred to for the whole, as when we say 'hands' in the sense of a group of workers, or 'This hotel is a favourite with all the crowned heads of Europe'. In the literary context we use the word metonymy for those comparisons in which the two terms belong or are close to each other, as the hands and heads belong to the sailors or monarchs they stand for in those everyday examples. The element of closeness, or contiguity, may consist of physical closeness in space, in the field of vision, or in generally available mental association. Thus in the examples we are considering, St Hilaire rising above the rest of Combray, lends to the hour of noon the quality of being 'altière' – haughty – (both words containing the idea of height); and the two golden marks on a blue curve, the heraldic sound-fleurets of the midday crown, the 'azure silence' itself, are all conjured up by the physical vision or the mental consciousness of the bell-tower against the sky. This fundamentally metonymic set of images may be contrasted with a later sentence in which the same ideas of the church-bell and of reading give rise to a comparison without the element of contiguity, a startling though serene personification:

Et j'aurais voulu pouvoir m'asseoir là et rester toute la journée à lire en écoutant les cloches; car il faisait si beau et si tranquille que, quand sonnait l'heure, on aurait dit non qu'elle rompait le calme du jour, mais qu'elle le débarrassait de ce qu'il contenait et que le clocher, avec l'exactitude indolente et soigneuse d'une personne qui n'a rien d'autre à faire, venait seulement – pour exprimer et laisser tomber les quelques gouttes d'or que la chaleur y avait lentement et naturellement amassées – de presser, au moment voulu, la plénitude du silence.   (p. 166)

And I would have liked to be able to sit down and stay there all day long, reading and listening to the bells; for the weather was so fine and all so peaceful that, when the hour struck, you might have said it was not interrupting the calm of the day, but discharging it of its contents; and that the bell-tower, with the leisurely and painstaking exactitude of a person with nothing else to do, had, just then, − to release and let fall the few golden drops that the heat had slowly and naturally accumulated in it − simply pressed, at the right moment, the fullness of the silence.

This is one of the most striking of the anthropomorphic metaphors in *Combray*. A personification is often implied in Proust's writing simply, for instance, by words such as 'the smile' applied to the effects of sunlight; but this sylph or giantess pressing their essence from the hours is a presence related to the household spirits who fill the rooms in Léonie's house with the exquisite fragrances of preserved fruits and fresh bread. We may contrast their august, invisible activities with those of 'nature herself' (p. 75 above), Nature as a kind of dressmaker, who has cut out the scalloped hawthorn leaves and embroidered the maybuds for the altar as if on a wedding-dress. She is evidently doomed to be rejected when the narrator compares her artistry in 'lavishing [the pink hawthorn] with these rosettes of a colour too sweet and too rustically overblown' with that of a naïve 'village shopkeeper [decorating] an altar of repose'. Pink is the colour 'which seems most obviously beautiful in children's eyes' because it suggests either delicious edibility (pink sugar biscuits, cream with crushed strawberries) or else party clothes (*Combray*, pp. 139–140). The extravaganza of the hawthorns is viewed critically almost as soon as it is completed, and we are forewarned of a maturing of taste and sensibility which coincides with the ending of *Combray*.

In the last quotation above, the phrase 'on aurait dit' − you might have said − corresponds to 'comme' − 'like', or 'as', which introduce a simile rather than a metaphor. It is already apparent that Proust makes no such distinction, and alludes to most figures of speech as metaphor.

In certain passages, which tend to be those where metaphor is used to define personality or situation, we would prefer to speak of it as conceit − and in its bold interweaving of human dignity with imagery it is then often suggestive of conversational exuberance. A witty extravaganza of this kind, remaining closely in contact with its starting-point in the invalid's psychology, is used to characterise the inner life of Léonie. It may serve as an illustration, not only of a Proustian conceit, but also of the general problems of translating this style at its most inventive.

A conceit and its form

Si la journée du samedi, qui commençait une heure plus tôt et où elle était privée de Françoise, passait plus lentement qu'une autre pour ma tante, elle en attendait pourtant le retour avec impatience depuis le commencement de la semaine, comme contenant toute la nouveauté et la distraction que fût encore capable de supporter son corps affaibli et maniaque. Et ce n'est pas cependant qu'elle n'aspirât parfois à quelque plus grand changement, qu'elle n'eût de ces heures d'exception où l'on a soif de quelque chose d'autre que ce qui est, et où ceux que le manque d'énergie ou d'imagination empêche de tirer d'eux-mêmes un principe de rénovation demandent à la minute qui vient, au facteur qui sonne, de leur apporter du nouveau, fût-ce du pire, une emotion, une douleur; où la sensibilité, que le bonheur a fait taire comme une harpe oisive, veut résonner sous une main, même brutale, et dût-elle en être brisée; où la volonté, qui a si difficilement conquis le droit d'être livrée sans obstacle à ses désirs, à ses peines, voudrait jeter les rênes entre les mains d'événements impérieux, fussent-ils cruels. Sans doute, comme les forces de ma tante, taries à la moindre fatigue, ne lui revenaient que goutte à goutte au sein de son repos, le réservoir était trop long à remplir, et il se passait des mois avant qu'elle eût ce léger trop-plein que d'autres dérivent dans l'activité et dont elle était incapable de savoir et de décider comment user. Je ne doute pas qu'alors — comme le désir de la remplacer par des pommes de terre béchamel finissait au bout de quelque temps par naître du plaisir même que lui causait le retour quotidien de la purée dont elle ne se 'fatiguait' pas — elle ne tirât de l'accumulation de ces jours monotones auxquels elle tenait tant, l'attente d'un cataclysme domestique, limité à la durée d'un moment, mais qui la forcerait d'accomplir une fois pour toutes un de ces changements dont elle reconnaissait qu'ils lui seraient salutaires et auxquels elle ne pouvait d'elle-même se décider. Elle nous aimait véritablement, elle aurait eu plaisir à nous pleurer; survenant à un moment où elle se sentait bien et n'était pas en sueur, la nouvelle que la maison était la proie d'un incendie où nous avions déjà tous péri et qui n'allait plus bientôt laisser subsister une seule pierre des murs, mais auquel elle aurait eu tout le temps d'échapper sans se presser, à condition de se lever tout de suite, a dû souvent

hanter ses espérances comme unissant aux avantages secondaires de
lui faire savourer dans un long regret toute sa tendresse pour nous
et d'être la stupéfaction du village en conduisant notre deuil,
courageuse et accablée, moribonde debout, celui, bien plus précieux,
de la forcer au bon moment, sans temps à perdre, sans possibilité
d'hésitation énervante, à aller passer l'été dans sa jolie ferme de
Mirougrain, où il y avait une chute d'eau.   (p. 116)

Though my aunt's day began an hour earlier on Saturdays, when she
was also deprived of Françoise, so that it passed more slowly than
any other day for her, she could not help looking forward impatiently
to its coming round, even from the start of the week, as containing
all the novelty and eventfulness that her enfeebled and unstrung
physique was still in a condition to tolerate. Yet it was not the case
that she never hoped for any greater change, or that she knew none
of those hours in which we thirst for something other than what we
have, and when people whose lack of energy or imagination prevents
them from finding the source of renewal in themselves must implore
from the coming minute, from the postman's ring at the doorbell,
some novelty, even if it should be the worst, say a violent emotion
or a grief; in which the power of feeling, muted by contentment like
a harp left idle, longs to resound at the touch of a hand, even a
brutal hand, even a touch that shatters; and when the will, having
won at great cost the right to the unimpeded enjoyment of its desires
and its sorrows, would gladly abandon the reins to imperious events,
however cruel. No doubt, as my aunt's strength ran dry at the
slightest exertion and returned to her drop by drop in a state of rest,
the reservoir took too long to fill, and months went by before she
could experience the modicum of excess [of energy] others divert
into activity, and which she was incapable of knowing, or deciding,
how to use. I have no doubt that then − just as the wish to
substitute potatoes in béchamel sauce would arise after a certain time
from the very pleasure she derived from the daily recurrence of the
potato purée she 'never tired of' − she drew from the accumulation
of these monotonous days which meant so much to her the expectation of a domestic upheaval, one that would last only for a moment,
but would force her to make a change such as she knew might be
beneficial to her and which she could not, of her own accord, make
up her mind to. She really loved us, she would have mourned us with
pleasure; if it came about at a moment when she felt well and was
not in a perspiration, the news that a fire had broken out in which
we had all burned to death, that there would shortly be not a wall
of the house left standing, but that she had plenty of time to escape
at leisure on condition that she got up immediately, must often have
haunted her hopes as combining with the minor advantages of letting
her dwell on all her tender affection for us in a long regret, and be

the wonder of the village as chief mourner at our funerals, – brave, though bowed down with grief, upright though at death's door – the far more precious one [i.e advantage] of forcing her at the right moment, with no time to lose, no possibility of exhausting indecision, to go and spend the summer at Mirougrain, her pretty farm-house, where there was a waterfall.

The shortcomings of this English rendering are glaring, but in the main they illustrate grammatical peculiarities of general interest. The displeasing repetition of 'which' is practically unavoidable in the second sentence ('hours in which') and in the succession of statements about the fire, unless we have recourse to the somewhat strained rearrangement of the syntax as above. In French the words requiring to be translated as 'which' or 'in which' are more discreet – '*où*' and '*qui*' – and moreover take on different forms according to their grammatical function, so that where English must repeat 'when' and 'which' in the early part of the above passage, French has '*quand*', varying to its relative form '*où*', and '*qui*' also in the forms '*que*', '*auquel*', '*dont*' and so forth. Although the main words of the vocabulary have practically the same forms in both languages, often Latinate, poly-syllabic and economically conveying equivalent meanings, the entire phrasing and grouping, with verb-forms, punctuation and connective words demands minute rearrangement, failing which the effect in translation is of such intolerable stiffness that no reader can be expected to follow the development of the thought, let alone gain a notion of what all the fuss is about.

All this would be likely to apply to most translation from French into English, but Proust's writing is a complicated case. One of the outstanding differences between French and English syntax is the availability in the former of pronouns relating to nouns either before they occur in the text or at some distance away, after their occurrence. This is made possible by the fact that the gender of nouns is reflected in their pronouns as well as in the adjectives and participles attached to them. The use Proust makes of this flexibility is audacious and notorious, and is one of the features of his writing that incurs, or has incurred, condemnation from

French purists. The ideal of French style is clarity, and in the usage of classical French writers the variety of phrasing made possible by the gender of pronouns, among other forms, is combined with and contributes to that clarity. There is no doubt that Proust's sentences occasionally oblige every reader, French or foreign, to reread before being able to establish the relationships between their clauses. In this passage about Léonie the virtuosity of the writing takes a while to declare itself; speculation begins with some more or less conventional expressions, dead metaphors presenting no problems of comprehension, even, perhaps, giving off a slightly stale, fruity odour like the odour of Léonie's counterpane by which Marcel likes to feel engulfed. These are:

où l'on a soif de — when we thirst for

comme une harpe oisive . . . brisée — like a harp left idle . . . shattered

jeter les rênes — to cast the reins

les forces . . . taries . . . goutte à goutte — her strength . . . ran dry . . . drop by drop.

We then arrive at a homely simile derived from potatoes. It is here we might expect to catch the first querulous tone from the academic critic of style; for the phrase '*la remplacer*' ('to replace *it*') suspends our need to find out what noun '*la*' refers to; glancing back at the preceding sentence will not help, since the last feminine noun is '*activité*', and the sense excludes this from the range of Léonie's wishes. When we, and our carping grammarian, discover that the noun referred to is the purée of potatoes fully three lines later, we may be amused, but he will probably become indignant. Lucidity is not well served by the intervening long phrase, to say nothing of the resistance in the French tradition to any intrusion of the ridiculously prosaic in such a context. Thus the analogy the narrator chooses for Léonie's supposed longing for a domestic disaster is established on the basis of a detail in her reassuringly boring daily round.

It must be a disaster, because nothing less will have the power to interrupt routine and compel a break with enslaving

habit. So the conceit emerges as Léonie's daydream of a con-
flagration, out of control when she hears of it and fatal to all
her family, including Marcel, but allowing her to escape with
dignity 'providing she gets out of bed at once'. The structure
of this main sentence alerts us early to the impending
extravaganza. Not once does the word 'paradoxical' occur,
though paradox is the fundamental idea from the very start
of the paragraph (longing for Saturday because it is both
interminable and eventful) and is apparent in the epigram,
reminiscent of Wilde, with which this sentence starts — 'She
really loved us, she would have mourned us with pleasure' —
and which is the take-off point for the long flight of fancy
that delights us as it is supposed by the narrator to delight
Léonie. The subject of the main clause is 'the news' of this
doubly chimærical fire (Léonie imagines it, or so the narrator
imagines), though its appearance is further delayed by the
subordinate clause stipulating its optimal timing. This news,
then, must often have haunted — not her thoughts but her
hopes, as combining the minor advantages of letting her bask
in 'the long regret' (again the slightly stale cliché appropriate
to Léonie) and by her heroic demeanour arouse the stupefac-
tion of the townspeople — but before proceeding to the
supreme and relatively simple 'advantage' that closes the
sentence, we must pause on a grammatical question without
waiting for our imaginary pedant to intervene.

The first of the two minor advantages is 'to let her savour'
or 'bask in' the fullness of her affection for her family. The
second is '*d'être la stupéfaction du village*', that is, 'be the
wonder of the village'. The English construction involves a
simple accusative with 'let', as we have no dative pronoun
such as '*lui*'. But in French, to make '*d'être la stupéfaction*'
depend on '*lui faire*', like the prevous clause, is impermissible,
and it is not too much to say that these words sound to a
French ear like an incorrect rendering from English. The
intoxication of this fundamentally conversational fantasy as
a whole involves a syntactical freedom which cannot be fully
available to the translator in English, and which, at least in
this detail, is eccentric in the French. A syntactically possible

but awkward version would be 'et de lui permettre d'être la stupéfaction' And yet this arrogated freedom corresponds in an entirely satisfactory way to the effect of a flight of fancy, the departure on the wings, as it were, both of the narrator's imagination and of Léonie's daydream. 'Her pretty farm, Mirougrain, where there was a waterfall' is the imagined haven, and the type of the lost paradise inaccessible to the neurasthenic invalid who can visit it only in thought. In this eccentric reverie, it becomes hard to distinguish Léonie from her nephew.

The canons of the French language demand precision in construction as a matter of course, but such infringements of them are strikingly common in *La Recherche*; the very next sentence contains a loose clause which it would be stretching tolerance to describe as parataxis. In some degree this characteristic results from Proust's insistence on developing an idea to its ultimate extent before arriving at a full stop. We become aware of an anxiety on the writer's part that the end of the sentence, sometimes even a semi-colon 'for breath', will bring about a failure to convey the whole 'vision' as it were simultaneously, as when a witty speaker or a dramatist delays the expected appreciation or applause until reaching a climactic point. In other contexts – for instance in descriptions of powerful visual impressions, like the passage in *Within a Budding Grove* when Marcel first sees the sea – the anxiety is rather to ensure that all aspects of the scene should be conveyed simultaneously to the reader as they were to the eyes of the protagonist. Thus what is seen, felt or imagined is modified in a rapid retouching of attendant and perhaps contradictory elements as though in defiance of the limitations of what can be done with language – what Lessing called the 'Nacheinander', or as we might say 'the rule of one thing at a time', to which all writing is in thrall. This anxiety to retouch, modify or re-embroider, while losing nothing of the elements first presented, is the analogy, in stylistics, to those revaluations in the moral sphere we have discussed, and to the revisions or revisitings of themes and judgments.

Chapter 4

Un Amour de Swann

An adult world

The opening of *Un Amour de Swann* transforms the pace and drift of the writing. The reader has the impression of embarking on a new novel, and the change is startling, perhaps even unwelcome. It is not only the virtual disappearance of the narrator that causes a sense of loss. *Combray*, for all its variety, has a smoothness of texture and an aesthetic harmony corresponding to the anchoring of the narrative self in the security of childhood, and this impression prevails over the melancholy or menacing notes of apprehension. In the final section of *Swann's Way* and in the middle volumes, a gentler transition is provided as Marcel's perception becomes once more the medium of the narrative, but the interruption constituted by *Un Amour de Swann* sounds a new note which is to recur in the last four volumes, when Marcel's own vision is that of an adult. Here the change is to a primarily social, sophisticated world in which a first phase of comic observation introduces the central exploration of Swann's inner life. It is an intense, gradually darkening study of obsession.

We are not prepared for this change at first reading, but it is retrospectively 'announced' very late in *La Recherche*, at the centre of *Time Regained*, when the narrator is returning to Paris from his sanatorium during the War. While the train is halted, he sees a row of trees, their trunks shaded by their sunlit foliage, and recalls the meaning, or rather the messages, such sights once had for him:

Arbres, vous n'avez plus rien à me dire, mon cœur refroidi ne vous entend plus . . . Si j'ai jamais pu me croire poète, je sais maintenant que je ne le suis pas. Peut-être dans la nouvelle partie de ma vie, si desséchée, qui s'ouvre, les hommes pourraient-ils m'inspirer ce que ne me dit plus la nature.   (vol. III, p. 855)

Trees, you can tell me nothing now, my heart, grown cold, has ceased to hear you . . . If I ever thought myself a poet, I know now I am not one. Perhaps in the new, so arid phase of my life, which is beginning, human beings might be able to inspire in me what nature no longer tells me.

Even as the narrator accepts the irretrievable loss of the poetic faculty, he is within a day or two of finding the way back to it, and the possibility of uniting it with his experience of human society. In the stages of the novel's development, however, this temporary farewell is really a prolonged drawing back, and it begins as *Combray* ends. Like all the other 'events' of *La Recherche*, whether intellectual or external, this ending is announced repeatedly, faintly or explicitly, and creates its own series of reminiscences like overlapping circles.

The name of Verdurin

The Verdurins and their set are first introduced in a way that would not seem surprising in a work by Balzac (it may remind us of his account of Mme de Bargeton's salon in *Illusions perdues*), except that the familiar technique has been speeded up, so that instead of occupying pages of dense information the result is achieved in two short paragraphs. The aims and the means of Mme Verdurin's system of hospitality, and her guest-list in the year of Swann's inclusion in it, are so rapidly conveyed that numerous brief quotations from dialogue can thereafter be employed to further the narration. This is a method we have already come to know in *Combray*, and as with the conversations between Léonie and Françoise, the imperfect tense of the verbs of speech introducing these quotations gives the desired effect of habitual and typical exchanges. It would be hard to imagine a more economical device for the characterisation of the speech-habits and general tone of a côterie. The method also serves to create in barely three pages an impression of a considerable span of years past, during which Mme Verdurin has established her salon as a kind of dining-club in which her vaunted contempt for all convention has become an iron rod of informality.

'The Verdurins did not issue invitations to dinner, there was just "a place at table for you".' The 'faithful' include a painter nicknamed Monsieur Biche, a pianist they call Ski, the rising young doctor, Cottard, and Brichot, a professor of literature. Only three women guests are tolerated, since women have been found sceptical of the charm of unadulterated Bohemianism. They are the doctor's wife, the pianist's aunt, 'qui devait avoir tiré le cordon' (i.e. who looked like an ex-concierge), and Mme Verdurin's favourite, Odette de Crécy. One other guest, the habitual butt of sneers and snubs − an Aunt Sally, or Turk's head as the French has it − is the archivist Saniette. With this list and this prevailing atmosphere, we may detect a more remarkable reminiscence than that noted in the scene-setting. Balzac's Mme Vauquer, the owner of a 'family boarding-house' with dinner for non-residents, in the seedy Faubourg St Marceau in Paris, rules her company tyrannically and regards absenteeism as a betrayal, though of course for commercial rather than social reasons. The pension Vauquer has among its clerks and medical students a number of professional humorists who, like Proust's Dr Cottard and the painter, deal in flattery of their hostess, facetious speech-mannerisms and frightful puns; and there, too, essential to the tactics of terror they all submit to, is the pathetic butt of cruel jokes called Père Goriot. Despite the superb cuisine and luxurious surroundings she offers, Mme Verdurin has greater need of her 'regulars' than they have of her, and in trying to disguise this need she reproduces with fidelity the behaviour of Balzac's grasping and base-minded Mme Vauquer.

After its brilliantly concise opening, the narration of *Un Amour de Swann* takes a step back from the action it has initiated, and indeed plunges the reader into the earliest period of time the novel deals with, for we are to learn of Swann's relationships with women before his meeting with Odette. There are later glimpses of the corresponding phase of her life too, but these are a matter of Swann's, and later Marcel's, divining facts from hints grudgingly conceded. The range of Swann's philanderings is reported in the style of third-person

authorial omniscience which forms the striking contrast between this part of the novel and the rest, though not without
a couple of glances back to the testimony of Marcel's grandparents – 'Look out! Here's Swann after something or
other!' (p. 66–7 above). Swann's pursuit of women has been
both ruthless and, in the matter of endings, adroit; his suc-
cesses in every sphere of society have left him unembarrassed
by complications. His cynicism infects the narrator with some
of its squalor when reporting, for instance, that Swann would
recklessly expend 'all his credit with a duchess' by suddenly
demanding of her a telegram of introduction to one of her
estate-managers whose daughter had taken his fancy. (We
recall Legrandin, and the peculiar marionette-like form of life
represented by duchesses in the account of his social
climbing.)

A certain intricacy of time-sequence still survives into the
account of Swann's first evening at the Verdurins; detailed
knowledge of their habits is not to be conveyed without brief
allusions, using the pluperfect tense, to the past events which
have given rise to these habits and made them into traditions.
Mme Verdurin, though she is constantly in a state of merri-
ment, never laughs, but buries her face in her hands and
shakes convulsively, because 'once' she laughed too heartily,
dislocated her jaw and had to have it put back by Dr Cottard.
Her husband vies with her in his appreciation of wit by puff-
ing and choking on his pipe. At the climax of this evocation
Mme Verdurin, perched on her high throne-like chair, is the
subject of a brief surreal conceit:

Thus, dizzy with the jollity of her devotees, tipsy with camaraderie,
malice and fellow-feeling . . . like a bird whose biscuit has been dip-
ped in mulled wine, [she] sobbed for very amiability.

After many interruptions caused by the need of indoct-
rinate Swann as rapidly as possible with the articles of faith,
the pianist sits down to play, and at once Swann himself is
returned to a past experience which requires to be announced
with the phrase 'Voici pourquoi' – 'The reason was as
follows' – which often heralds a long explanation in the
novels of Balzac (so typically, indeed, that Proust uses it

effectively in his pastiche of Balzac). What it introduces in this case is the delineation of Swann's inmost sensations when he heard *on a previous occasion* the piece of music for violin and piano of which the Verdurins' friend is *now* performing the piano rendering. The delight of recognition is half the pleasure of this new hearing, so the reader is to be enabled to participate in that delight. For three pages more (pp. 208–11) the narrative pauses on Swann's inner life, and on the immense renewal of it he has believed in, for a time, as the result of hearing the sonata once and once only – for he had then been unable to learn the composer's name, which he is now told is Vinteuil. Even the 'little phrase' of five notes, whose recurrence forms the greatest charm of the work for Swann, had proved too elusive for him to memorise. Now that he hears it again, the little phrase becomes profoundly associated with Odette. The pianist will play it whenever Swann arrives, and his fellow-guests accept it as one of their consecrated jokes – it is the signature-tune ('l'air national' as Odette says) of the love-affair that is beginning in Mme Verdurin's salon.

From this point onwards, however, the development of *Un Amour de Swann* is linear, hardly diverging from the chronological; it moves smoothly from one *state of things* to the next (rather than from one event to the next), with incidents illustrative of, or actually causing, each phase. Changes soon brought about in Swann are noted by his old friends, and they are first struck by his ceasing to chase after women, since Odette occupies all his attention. The torments Swann is to suffer through Odette conform, against the background of his former habits, to an old pattern of narration – the story of the seducer caught in his own toils, of Love's Vengeance or The Tables Turn'd.

This aspect of *Un Amour de Swann* generates the high comedy of the reversal that occurs months later when Mme Verdurin excludes Swann from her next party and neatly separates him from Odette at the end of an evening they have spent at a restaurant. Walking home alone through the Bois de Boulogne, Swann gives vent to his feelings in audible

monologue, the long wail of wounded pride. Months of happiness have reconciled him to all the absurdities of the
Verdurins, he has publicly committed himself to his new faith
(p. 67 above) – and now these absurdities rush back on him
in all their freshness, and are vindictively listed. The very name
of Verdurin is an enigma suddenly resolved ('quel nom!' –
what a name! he cries aloud) though the suggestion that has
lain dormant in its unfortunate syllables ('vert du rein' –
kidney-green perhaps) is left for the reader to articulate.
Odette's own failings, falsity, bad taste ('and above all, poor
little thing, she's so stupid!') – abruptly emerge from the
enchantment with which her lover's vanity has veiled them.

Swann cast out

The rival whom Swann knows to be dangerous is his acquaintance, the Comte de Forcheville, introduced into the Verdurin
clan by Odette just as Swann had been earlier; and, in spite
of his title, well received because his notion of humour and
good fellowship is far closer to that of the clan than Swann's;
Forcheville is sincerely impressed by Brichot's displays of
pedantry, and laughs wholeheartedly at Cottard's imbecile
jokes. Related by marriage to Saniette, Forcheville one evening tires of the presence of this witness from another sphere
of his existence, and attacks him with brutal sarcasms on the
pretext of some tactless remark, 'emboldened, the more he
shouted at him, by [Saniette's] alarm, his pain, his entreaties
[till] the unhappy man, having asked Mme Verdurin if he
should remain, and receiving no reply, left the house . . . with
tears in his eyes'.

The scene strongly suggests a kinship with scenes in the
novels of Nathalie Sarraute, where episodes of physical
violence are mentally 'enacted' between persons conversing in
an ostensibly civilised way in a drawing-room; no defence is
possible to the victims of such assaults, and the spectacle
draws in onlookers through a kind of blood-lust. For Swann
the significance of the incident is the sparkling glance of glee
and complicity with which Odette rewards Forcheville when

it is over — a look at variance with the gentle sympathy she has often expressed for the victims of cruelty. Because of this look, Swann's secure knowledge of her kindness and goodness is shaken, and when he is cast out from the clan he remembers Odette's response to the 'execution' of Saniette, and imagines her laughing with Forcheville over the piteous look on his own face as Mme Verdurin's carriage drove away with them. The impression made on others by Swann's physique, as well as his own sensations and habits, are a strong element in that 'precise knowledge' of him the narrator claims, and which he conveys to the reader. The coachman Rémi, catching sight of his master's face at the same moment, asks if he has been taken ill (the same look of sickness will warn Odette to try to take back a lie that has failed). Sending Rémi away, Swann walks home through the Bois in the dark; in his fury, grimacing with disgust, he is aware of the rigidity in the muscles of his neck as they tense against his shirt-collar, and the tone of his voice as he loudly denounces the Verdurins has the same artificiality it had when he was exalting their simplicity and magnanimity in the phase just past.

The comic view of Swann's inconsistencies does not long survive the account of this incident, though it lingers into the pages immediately following, as he inwardly wonders how Odette's bad taste can have resisted his influence so completely. She leaves him alone to go with the Verdurins to see *A Night with Cleopatra* at the Opéra-Comique, and later to visit a château restored by Viollet-le-Duc, and he tries to rationalise by aesthetic disapproval the suffering her desertion causes him. But in the phase of the affair which now opens, Swann's subservience to Odette becomes complete, and his love is compared by the narrator to the pathological condition of a person with tuberculosis, or that of a morphine addict. Comedy recedes before the solemnity of the case. Swann has wasted time, and wasted people too, and now time and Odette waste him.

The full recognition of Odette's venality — which, since he now obviously bores her, is his only real hold on her — prepares Swann for the truth about her behaviour in other ways. Her demands for money, which he resolves to resist but always gives in to for the sake of an hour or two of graciousness from her, are the essential element in the period of slow disillusionment; for Swann is dimly aware that his generiosity allows Forcheville, with the connivance of the Verdurins, to enjoy Odette's favours without paying for them. It is part of Swann's nature to spare himself the painfulness of the truth, so he avoids the tangible reminders of his past happiness for fear of the agonising comparison with the present that they would force him to make. However, 'his wary prudence was outwitted one evening when he went to a party'.

This musical evening given by the Marquise de Saint-Euverte is the only social occasion, since those Verdurin dinners, which relieves the monotony of Swann's miserable waiting on Odette's pleasure. It is also the first occurrence in the novel of Proust's expansive treatment of 'grand entertainments'. On the pretext of Swann's already well-established propensity to see human beings as figures in paintings, the reader is confronted with a set-piece − the three-page description (pp. 323–5), in terms of Renaissance art, of the Marquise's footmen and lackeys. Selected for their size and handsome features, lounging or standing to attention in the doorways and arches that give on to the monumental staircase, these hirelings bring to Swann's mind the models of Mantegna, Dürer and Cellini, and the Staircase of the Giants of the Palazzo Ducale in Venice; but they also recall by contrast the décor of another staircase, one that Swann would prefer to be climbing at that moment had Odette permitted him to do so. It is the evening she devotes to visiting an old dressmaker of hers, whose flat is up five flights, where, at night, dirty milk-cans wait on each landing to be filled next morning.

With a fresh vision − since he has not been out in society for so long − Swann appraises the ugliness of his fellow guests after the beauty of the serving-men, and becomes for a while obsessed with the monocles most of his acquaintances wear. His brief study of these adjuncts to various familiar faces is recorded with an unforgettable brilliance which none the less reflects the hypersensitivity from which he is suffering; General de Froberville wears his monocle like a facial wound which has been honourably suffered but is obscenely exhibited; M. de Palancy, who looks like a carp, seems to have a fragment of his glass aquarium stuck to his eye.

After the performance of several pieces − a flute solo from *Orpheus*, a Liszt piano intermezzo and a Chopin prelude − during which the music itself, and the varying responses of the guests to it, provide the material for a virtuoso introduction to this society, an interval occurs during which Swann notices his friend the Princesse des Laumes ('who was not yet' Mme de Guermantes). This first appearance (in the chronological sense) of the future Duchess is remarkable, as the introduction to the Verdurin milieu was, for the rapidity and confidence with which it is accomplished. It becomes possible to believe in the attraction exercised by her vain, spiteful and yet sparkling chatter, and to understand the fear she inspires in other women.

In reply to a compliment from General de Froberville, she says 'People always talk about "the wit of *the* Guermantes". Does it mean you know some *others* who make you laugh?' − and bursts out laughing herself, 'her features concentrated, merging in the network of her animation, eyes shining, aflame with a radiant sunlight of gaiety which was only capable of being set beaming like this by a remark, even one she made herself, that contained praise of her wit or of her beauty.'

This sentence, with its effect of containing fragments of metaphor rather than of being a metaphor, is typical of the images with which *Un Amour de Swann* abounds, and which are so different in kind from the leisurely extended analogies of *Combray* that they seem to correspond to the more mature, less literary sensibility that is Swann's own, compared with the dreamy playfulness of Marcel's. No less striking, but briefer, deriving from psychological insights rather than from sensuous experience, such images are the precise correlative in the writing to that explicit farewell to the poetic

immersion of the self in nature quoted above (p. 96) —
'Arbres, vous n'avez plus rien à me dire.'

Swann's dialogue with the Princess is vivacious, for she
greets him with delight as the only member of her own set at
Mme de Saint-Euverte's party, but for him the value of their
talk is in a rather banal remark of hers about life being
frightful — he seizes on it as a sign of sympathetic understanding: 'the lovely thing about you is that you're not cheer-
ful', he tells her gratefully.

The music is resumed before Swann can carry out his intention of leaving this house where, as he is dismally aware,
Odette is, and always will be, unknown. But suddenly

it was as if she had entered, and the apparition caused him such
acute pain that involuntarily he put his hand to his heart. . . . The
violin had risen to high notes and held them as if waiting, went on
waiting in the exaltation of perceiving the object of its waiting
already approaching, and with a desperate effort to last till it arrived,
to welcome it before expiring, to keep the way open for a moment
longer so that it could pass through, as one holds back a door which
would otherwise swing shut. And before Swann had had time to
understand, and to say to himself 'It's the little phrase from
Vinteuil's sonata, don't let's listen!', all his memories of the time
when Odette was in love with him . . . had reawakened . . . and had
soared up to sing to him wildly . . . the forgotten choruses of
happiness.

The next passage of two pages occupies no 'real time'. It
describes the instantaneous release of all the 'specific and
volatile essence' of past happiness — involuntary memory
floods past the defences of his will, and Swann stands helpless,
seeing himself overwhelmed like a pitiable stranger with his
eyes full of tears: 'on the misted surface of his monocle, with
a handkerchief, he was trying to wipe away his sadness'. The
evocation of the music itself follows, while Swann penetrates
into a different state, almost achieving that rejuvenation of
his whole being which he had believed in when he first heard
the little phrase. In part his experience during these moments
is reflective, in part emotional. The little phrase of five notes,
which has caused him such agony, becomes a consoling deity,
whispering to him of Odette among the indifferent crowd

about him and making light of his sorrows, while at the same time giving voice to them as if they were the only thing in the world worthy to be thought of: 'No doubt the form in which it had codified them [his sorrows] was incapable of being resolved into arguments.' But for Swann his still recent apprenticeship in music has revealed the power of themes to convey ideas — impenetrable to the intelligence, but distinct in value. For the first time he now thinks with pity and sympathy of Vinteuil himself, and wonders what sorrows enabled him to create like a god. (We know what they were, and so does Swann, but he cannot associate his present spiritual experience with the man he has always thought of as a pathetic old fellow at Combray). Swann knows that the piano-scale of seven notes falsifies his idea of music, which is 'an immeasurable keyboard, as yet almost entirely unknown', where great artists have discovered some few of the millions of notes of tenderness, passion, courage, serenity to show us what wealth, what variety is concealed by 'the great impenetrable, discouraging' darkness of our soul which we mistake for void and nothingness. For Swann, and for those who heard it with him, Vinteuil's little phrase was 'so explicit' that they retained it in their minds like their notions of the particularity of certain works of literature, but also like their notions of light, of sound or of physical pleasure, 'the rich possessions of our inner domain'. These, says the voice which mediates Swann's experience to us, are the hostages, the divine captives which espouse our mortal condition and are bound to the 'reality of our souls':

Et la mort avec elles a quelque chose de moins amer, de moins inglorieux, peut-être de moins probable. (p. 350)

And death, with them, is a thing less bitter, less inglorious, perhaps less probable.

Thus it is that the precautions Swann has taken against being forced to confront his true emotional situation are outwitted, and from this moment he ceases to hope for the return of Odette's love.

Lies

The ensuing phase of Swann's affair with Odette is the most infernal of all. His new honesty is partly responsible for a new scepticism in which he sees through the lies she tells him, without being any nearer to the truths the lies are meant to conceal. At times some fact reveals itself in spite of her, and has to be patched into the tissue of mendacity already woven; on other occasions, Swann startles her into admissions he has not dreamed of, by pretending to know more than he has been told. An anonymous letter, which he fears may be from some friend, warns him against Odette, listing her past lovers, including Forcheville and the painter Biche (whom Marcel will later meet as Elstir), and accusing her of lesbianism and of going to 'maisons de passe' – that is, to the establishments of professional procuresses. None of these offences rings true, for Swann cannot reconcile them with the daily actions he sees Odette going through when they are together, or with her professions of distaste for indelicacy. Yet a chance association of words reminds him of a reference Odette had made two years earlier to the affection Mme Verdurin was in the habit of demonstrating to her; and because of the anonymous letter he determines to question her about her relations with women. He does this so deviously that Odette is convinced he has definite information, and after an angry scene she concedes that she may have 'done things of that kind . . . two or three times'. It is the last reply Swann expects, and the words – 'words pronounced in the air, at a distance' – cut into his heart in what he feels as a wound like a cross. As soon as he can speak, he resumes his questions, and details follow. The idea that words can inflict a mortal illness occurs several times during this dialogue, as Swann receives more and more cruel blows from Odette's complaint answers. When on a later occasion he asks her about procuresses, still feeling certain that this accusation, at least, is impossible, Odette at once tells him that though she always refuses what they ask, she is constantly 'persecuted' by the attentions of these women, and was only the day before visited by one, who entreated her to consent to a meeting with a foreign ambassador. Odette's vanity vies with her mendacity and begins to produce an infinity of discrepant accounts of incidents from what were, for Swann, their happiest times. The pain of 'the happy memory in days of sadness' is rendered intolerable when the happy memory turns out to have been a lie. These wretched fragments of confessions, often recanted as soon as spoken, obsess Swann: 'son âme les charriait, les rejetait, les berçait comme des cadavres' – 'his mind bore them along, tossed them up, rocked them like corpses'.

This image, here given in its entirety, belongs, in its economy (no 'dark river' needs to be alluded to, but the reader's inward eye sees it flowing) to the same family as the evocation of the Princess's laughter (p. 104 above). But in *Un Amour de Swann* the most remarkable of such images are devoid of visual expansiveness, and even remoter from the gentle facility of metonymy – they seem wrenched from suffering, brief like an involuntary groan.

In a rare concession to the manner of conventional realism, we are informed of the factual background to a development in the narrative which is to bring about the eventual healing of Swann's obsession:

As the painter had been ill, Dr Cottard advised a sea-voyage; several of the faithful talked of going too; the Verdurins could not bear to be left alone, rented a yacht, and then purchased it, and thus Odette often went off on cruises.

This 'explanation', somewhat impatient though it sounds, is one of the very few exceptions to the general rule of merely parenthetic glances at circumstance, which prevails in this part of the book as much as in *Combray*. It even entails a further short factual account of the Mediterranean itinerary of the longest cruise, which lasts almost a year, and with some earlier references to dates establishes the duration – somewhat over three years – of Swann's love for Odette. This admittedly minor departure from the practice we have become used to suggests that third-person narration and authorial omniscience might have tended to undermine Proust's determination to avoid the recital of invented 'facts', which he regarded as one of the outstanding defects of the realistic novel.

The causes of things are almost always taken up only as they have to be woven into the narrator's consciousness (see p. 69 above), usually after their occurrence. Generally this has been the case in the study of Swann's experience too, but a point may be reached where a kind of artificiality declares itself in the attempt to incorporate *events* by this method, to treat his consciousness subjectively as if it were continuous with the narrator's own.

In Odette's long absence Swann begins to understand that he is ceasing to suffer on her account, and when he admits it to himself, the process of recovery is already accomplished.

The type of Odette

Swann first meets Odette at the theatre, introduced to her by a friend who has described her as more '*difficile*' – more selective – in her choice of lovers than she really is. Her appearance, though striking, fails to impress Swann, because her huge sad eyes, poor complexion and strong profile are in contrast to the fresh, carefree look of the girls who usually appeal to his senses. For a time, Odette has to make all the advances: calling often on her new acquaintance, admiring his erudition, asking about his study of Vermeer (of whom she has never previously heard), and offering the flattery of her submissive availability whenever Swann is free to see her. In this phase he still regrets that she is not more attractive, but he begins to treasure her naïveté and bad taste, even her greed for money, as elements of authenticity – if she were more perceptive or better educated she would not be true to type as '*une cocotte*'. A decisive moment in the early phase of their relationship occurs when Swann 'recognises' in Odette another type, the physical type of Botticelli's preferred models, and in particular the painting of Zephora, Jethro's daughter. (Similarly, his coachman Rémi has the features of the doge Loredano in the portrait by Antonio Rizzo, and

Marcel's friend Bloch is 'placed', as soon as Swann sees him, by his close resemblance to the Sultan Mahomet II painted by Bellini). Once this recognition has taken effect, Odette's features acquire nobility and are assimilated to Swann's cult of the aesthetic. No longer a mere woman, she shares the qualities of a Florentine painting, and instead of regretting the months of his life he has devoted to her to the exclusion of friends and study, he can justify himself on the grounds that his time is given to a masterpiece.

The narrator associates Swann's dilettantism in relation to Odette – his tendency to think of her as an object – with Marcel's own yearnings, at Combray, to meet some ardent peasant-girl who would emerge like a plant from her natural surroundings, an emanation of the woods. But this adolescent dream is very innocent compared with the spurious move which enables Swann to deceive his own intelligence – his delusion, that is, that he 'possesses' in Odette something of what he appreciates in the art of Botticelli. At the end of *Un Amour de Swann*, when after his long thralldom he begins to recover from 'the illness that was his love', Swann wakes one morning from a heartbreaking dream of a lost freshness of emotion and recalls that, in the dream, Odette's drawn face and heavy eyes had been accurately reproduced by his memory although no longer present in his conscious image of her. It is then that he reproaches himself, in words that have become celebrated, for having wasted years of his life on a woman he did not find attractive – 'qui n'était pas mon genre!' – who was not his type.

The narrator's introductory comment on this is important: it is an example of 'the boorishness (*la muflerie*) which would reassert itself in him as soon as he ceased to feel unhappy, when simultaneously his morality sank to a lower level' – a failure to understand his own nature, which the reader can by this time associate with Swann's habitual refusal, from indolence, to pursue any taxing train of thought. In this instance, what he is failing to grasp is that our affections are not engaged by the type of beauty or of moral worth which appeals to our senses or our detached judgment. Desire is aroused by the circumstances of encounters, by 'anticipations' of the kind we have observed in *Combray*, where intellectual images collect about the name of someone yet unknown, and by mystery. Since we can never fully know another person, or be certain about everything they do ('the residue of time which, even in days fully detailed, still leaves some free play, some space' [p. 371]), mystery inevitably arises, and is the potent origin of love. This idea is most concisely and, indeed, poetically expressed when the narrator tells us that the beginning of an obsessive passion can often be traced to a phrase such as 'Non, ce soir je ne serai pas libre' — 'No, I shan't be free this evening.' Not to have acknowledged the fundamental truth that love is not governed by our reason, to have been too indolent to identify it in all the course of his affair with Odette, is what constitutes the 'boorishness' of Swann.

An interesting aspect of this ending of *Un Amour de Swann* is suggested by the words above, 'as soon as he ceased to feel unhappy'. The dream of Odette is a farewell to Swann's love, arranged as it were by his subconscious mind; for some time previously he has felt a nostalgia even for the acute sufferings of jealousy, aware that with his recovery from the malady of love he is losing the intensity of emotion in which he has lived as though in a strange country. On the morning when he awakes from the dream, he is to leave for a visit to Combray after a long absence — for in his obsessive fear of missing a rare glimpse of Odette he has been tied to Paris even when she is elsewhere. In a manner that is casual rather than parenthetic — for the subject occupies a full page — we are informed of the immediate reason for this departure: Swann has already written to the narrator's grandfather to announce his arrival in Combray, 'having learned that Mme de Cambremer' — (Legrandin's sister) — 'was to be there for a few days'. Just as he had often remembered his first sight of Odette and how it meant nothing to him, Swann has been recalling of late the evening party at Mme de Saint-Euverte's when he last encountered Mme de Cambremer, as though it had the quality of 'a presentiment or a presage'. At the party, Swann's mood had been one of settled misery, yet he now perceives a kind of fated connection between the agonies he then felt on Odette's account and 'the still unsuspected pleasures which were already coming to life'.

What makes these hints unmistakable is the detail of the letter to the narrator's grandfather. Swann is in fact embarking on yet another adventure, 'associating the charm of [Mme de Cambremer's] young face with that of a landscape' and informing his country neighbours of his arrival in case their invitations may be of use in the furtherance of his plans. ('En garde! Watch out! Here's Swann after something or other!')

But no more is heard of Swann's designs on Mme de Cambremer (except for a rather mocking reference to her by Odette in *A l'Ombre des jeunes filles en fleurs*, which, as Marcel observes, calls up a momentary look of coy vanity on Swann's face). No account of the circumstances that obliged Swann to marry precedes his 'reappearance' in the guise of Odette's husband, which is of course his previous appearance, in *Combray*; there is only the briefest of references to the general belief that he did it for the sake of Gilberte, that is after her birth.

The story of Swann's love for Odette thus ends at the opening of a lacuna, a period which apparently remains obscure to the narrator; there is a gulf between the figure of Swann as we last see him here, liberated from the obsession with Odette and no longer even regretting his chains, and the new servitude in which he is held, in *Noms de pays: le nom* and in *Combray*, by his marriage and by fatherhood.

Noms de pays: le nom

The last short section of *Swann's Way* returns the reader to a time very shortly following on that of the end of *Combray*, after Léonie's death, and there is an end of the linear, omniscient technique used in *Un Amour de Swann*. This technique is by no means conventional, since, as has been said, that account moves on from one state of things, or rather of mind, to the next, instead of moving from one event to another; but it is suggestive none the less of a certain disciplined submission to facts which are to be imparted in order. The musing discursiveness of the narrator, remembering a past that is his own to arrange as he pleases, now resumed. Its first assertion of freedom is the curious leap forward in time to the hotel-room at Balbec in which Marcel will find himself some hundreds of pages *later*, recalled as one of the décors that haunted the sleeper in the bed some hundreds of pages *earlier*, at the beginning of *La Recherche*. Not only is Balbec thus part of the narrator's memories — the room with its low glazed bookcases reflecting the sea outside, and its rather unwelcoming look as of a 'modern style' furniture exhibition — but its *expected* qualities (wild, legendary, magical), as they existed in Marcel's imagination before he ever went there, are also summoned up in these opening paragraphs as vividly as the features of the real place, and set beside these at considerably more length. It is not bedroom furniture, as at the opening of the book, but the furniture of the mind, that is here made to 'whirl about' us, the readers.

The promise of an Easter holiday in Northern Italy fills Marcel's mind with visions of Florence and Venice, and of the works of art he will see there, adding another dimension to his dreams of places. The density of these evocations is their essential feature. There is scarcely enough room, in a name, for 'the elements which usually compose a city', and hardly more room for 'duration' — so Marcel is obliged to put together a 'supernatural' Florence, in which masses of flowers co-exist with scenes painted by Giotto. Like some of those scenes (e.g. incidents from different periods of a saint's life), this city is divided into two compartments, two simultaneous pictures which incorporate Marcel's own figure as participant and spectator. In one, Marcel is contemplating a sunlit fresco; in the other, he is hurrying across the Ponte Vecchio past heaps of jonquils and anemones, towards his lunch of fruit and Chianti.

We note the recurrence of what Sartre has called the 'mechanistic', and what we have preferred to describe as the child-like treatment of a psychological phenomenon, and note also that it is uniquely appropriate for its purpose.

Something resembling a theory of names emerges, or is to be derived, from this part of the book. But, as the reader by now expects, it is not really a theory at all, but a group of absolutely original observations based on images — not literary figures of speech, but the mind's images of physical experience. The force of this physicality emphasises above all the individual particularity names bestow on places as much as on people, and which constitutes the difference between *names* and mere *words*. The vague image conjured up by a place-name is compared by the narrator to an effect of colour 'like one of those posters, entirely blue or entirely red, in which . . . not only the sky and the sea are blue or red, but the boats, the church, and the people in the street'. The colour our minds give to places is attributed at this point to the brilliant or sombre sound of their names. This suggests the correspondence between resonance and impression, an idea which led to the ancient debate on the 'rightness' or necessary relationship of names to things — but this idea has been rejected in advance, with the observation that the names of things are mere words. The difference between words and names is to be seen as reminiscent of the difference between voluntary and involuntary memory, the functional and the poetic. And it is clear from Marcel's notions of Florence before he goes there that the narrator's argument relies on associations and intellectual knowledge *combined* with resonance to explain the potency of place-names. This is strikingly demonstrated again when he remembers that the name Parma, in his thoughts, seemed 'compact, smooth, mauve [i.e. violet-coloured] and sweet', and that this heavy, airless syllable ('Parme' in French) had absorbed, with the reflection of violets, all the sweetness of his *reading* of Stendhal's *Chartreuse de Parme*.

However, the railway time-tables, with their precise indications of hours and destinations, are to form Marcel's only acquaintance with new places for some years to come, because he falls ill and the doctor forbids all thought of travel or even of visits to the theatre. Now the only distraction allowed is the daily visit to the Champs-Elysées gardens with Françoise, and it is in this humdrum playground that once

more the name of Gilberte is heard, called by one of her
friends just as Marcel notices the red-haired girl playing
shuttlecock. Like the sound of the violin playing the little
phrase of Vinteuil's sonata, the voice seems to travel visibly
through the air; it trails a small cloud of precious hue above
the children and the nursemaids — a cloud formed of the
emanation from Gilberte's mysterious life, like a stage-cloud
reflecting the lives of the divinities on Olympus.

From this moment until six pages from the end, the narration of *Noms de pays: le nom* becomes linear as the story of
Swann's love-affair was linear, and within the framework of
adolescence resembles that story strongly. The likelihood of
Gilberte's presence in the gardens becomes the overwhelming
interest of Marcel's life, and the state of the weather, consequently, his main study. As Swann wished he could visit
Odette's old seamstress in her dreary apartment, Marcel longs
to be better acquainted with an old lady who is always sitting
in the gardens, because Gilberte speaks to her as a friend of
her mother's. Like Swann preserving a flower Odette gave
him, Marcel treasures one or two objects which come to him
from Gilberte. Swann himself figures in this period when
he comes to fetch his daughter home, causing Marcel some
difficulty in reconciling the knowledge he has of Swann as a
family friend and as the intimate of the exiled claimants to the
French throne, with the painfully inaccessible mystery of his
power, as her father, over Gilberte:

since the ideas I now attached to his name were different . . . he had
become a new person; but I joined him up by a secondary, artificial
and transversal line to our guest of former times —

remembering with shame how often Swann had been present
when he, Marcel, had sent imploring messages to his mother
to come upstairs to him at Combray. Now, too, the theme of
Swann's name as a source of somewhat guilty joys recurs ('it
[the name] had ceased to seem innocent to me') as Marcel
ingeniously arranges conversations with his parents in such a
way that they will have to utter it — and the anticipation of
this theme in *Combray* seems almost a dislocation, as the
narrator appears to have forgotten it.

The lure of Gilberte's mother is stronger still, and when the daughter is out of reach, Marcel asks Françoise to take him to the Bois de Boulogne, where Odette usually drives or walks in the fashionable afternoon procession. Her beauty, her stunning clothes and her reputation make her appearances something of a sensation, whether she is on foot and simply dressed, or reclining, theatrically accoutred, in her 'incomparable' high victoria, driven by a huge coachman and attended by a tiny groom who reminds Marcel of the mid-nineteenth century 'tigers', as such grooms are called in the novels of Balzac and Dickens. The remarks of some gentlemen one day as Odette passes ('I remember I was in bed with her the day of MacMahon's resignation' says one, astonished at her youthful looks) are reproduced by the narrator though Marcel does not hear them; he is getting ready to make an immense bow in Odette's direction, so exaggerated that she smiles despite herself. L'Allée des Acacias − the Acacia Walk − is the Zoological Garden of Women among all the other small distinct gardens of the Bois, and the spell of his love for Gilberte makes the precocious Marcel one of the loitering admirers of famous beauties there.

The last six pages of *Noms de pays: le nom*, though immediately connected with the foregoing scene, are entirely outside its framework. The boy Marcel and his chaperone Françoise abruptly disappear, and the adult narrator with the equally abrupt phrase 'cette année' − 'this year' − rises up more or less on the same spot in the Bois, a time-traveller making a ghost of his former self and of all that surrounded him as it were a moment before. The words 'this year' are as problematic as any in the novel, and oblige us to recall the quotation from Gérard Genette about narrative norms being overturned by Proust 'perhaps without even knowing it' (see above, pp. 10–11). To judge by his melancholy mood and the comments about his age which he addresses to himself, we are seeing the narrator in the very period of our first acquaintance with him; he is aimless and discouraged, more like Charles Swann than he has seemed before. If, then, to put it briefly, we must suppose that no revelation of the truth of involuntary memory

has yet visited him, why 'this year' (suggesting as it does the
time of writing)? Or if that revelation has occurred, even if
it has not yet enabled him to recognise his vocation, how
is it possible for him to mourn so heart-rendingly over
irrevocable loss as he does in the next few pages? For, with
a slightly apologetic reference to the 'fetichism' of our attachment to the old things we remember, the narrator proceeds to
a threnody devoted to the disappearance of the little hats, the
cluttered, intimate, sombre style of interior decoration, and
the elegant horse-drawn carriages that were Odette's. These
regrets, and even more the horror he expresses at what has
replaced these artefacts — big flowered hats, draped Liberty
chiffons, all-white apartments with blue hydrangeas in them
and, of course, motor-cars — these emotions for once leave
us as readers somewhat out of sympathy with him. The
resentment and the railing against fate are uncharacteristic;
the apology for fetichism is felt to have been all too necessary;
and the mourning for the past has become that of any ageing
person refusing to be reconciled to change.

It is in keeping with this feeling of disappointment that we
may find in the last sentence of *Swann's Way* a rather false
musicality and a weak comparison:

le souvenir d'une certaine image n'est que le regret d'un certain
instant; et les maisons, les routes, les avenues, sont fugitives, hélas!
comme les années.   (p. 427)

the memory of a particular image is only regret for a particular
moment; and houses, roads and avenues flee away, alas! like the
years or: are as fleeting, alas! as the years.]

The English translation sounds flat; so does the original.
'Fugitives' is not a happy adjective for houses, roads and
avenues. The language is infected with the sterility of the
lament, and the intended 'inevitability' of this last phrase is
not the inevitability of poetry, but is weary and perfunctory.
To confirm this impression it is well to return to a page of
Combray (p. 165) where reflections of a similar kind are given
a very different form. Setting out on the way to Guermantes,
Marcel and his parents would pass through the Rue des
Perchamps, whose strange name seemed to him responsible

for its surly personality. The narrator tells us that the street has disappeared long since beneath the buildings of Combray's new school, but he, in his thoughts of it, can remove the school stone by stone and restore the Rue des Perchamps with the help of –

some images preserved by my memory, the last perhaps that still exist, and destined soon to be wiped out, of what Combray was in my childhood . . . and which are emotionally powerful – if an obscure likeness can be compared to these glorious effigies – like old engravings of the Last Supper, or like the painting by Gentile Bellini, in which there can be seen, in a state that no longer exists, Leonardo's masterpiece and the great door of St Mark's.

These images are 'destined soon to be wiped out' – that is, by the narrator's own death. Yet in this sober comparison of the role of memory with that of art – oddly precise and factual, like Swann's contributions to aesthetic discussions – and the acknowledgement of the absolute loss that has overtaken the Rue des Perchamps of the past, there is no vestige of the self-pity and resentment which estranges the reader in the lament over the Bois de Boulogne.

The miscalculation of the effect of these last paragraphs of *Swann's Way* was the reason for Proust's wishing he could rewrite them, changing their mood and their message so that they should be in harmony with the deeply felt and long-meditated serenity of the novel's conclusion in *Time Regained*.

Chapter 5

The reception of Proust's novel

At night, with electricity economised, the place is entirely dark, and at first, among the many entrances that open on all sides of the court-yard, I would always become confused and have to summon the *portiere*. You need matches to achieve the ascent of the shallow and wide and deep interminable marble stairs, made for unimaginable grandeur, that the proportionately lofty arched windows illuminate only faintly; and by the glimmer, beneath the stone vaults and among the great funeral vases and the flower-carved entablatures, one has glimpses of Roman relics that appear, on their heroic scale, in a completely Surrealist key; the conventionally statuesque pose of a white naked hero with a sword would be followed by a similar figure in an unexpected half-squatting posture; a single finger from an ancient colossus, standing upright on a pedestal, loomed as tall as an ordinary statue; and a bearded man, seated . . . and leaning forward intent on a book, had the appearance of reading in the toilet. As the staircase goes on so long that you finally lose count of the landings, you are likely to try wrong apartments and get the rooms of some lurking nobleman whose old butler peers out through the crack of a door apprehensively secured by a chain.

From 'Rome in Midsummer' in *Europe without Baedeker* by
Edmund Wilson (1948)

Slipshod though this writing is, it also represents a style and a vision of things which is hardly to be found before the influence of Proust began to spread. As an example of that influence it is more important than examples from writers who announce an intention of paying homage to it, and who address themselves to explicitly Proustian themes – important just because it is almost a random choice from a not very literary work by an author of wide culture but only moderate distinction. We can say with confidence that 'we' have learned to see in this way because Edmund Wilson is not unlike most educated readers. We may guess that in seeing the Roman stairway as he does, he is directly if not consciously influenced by the 'Giants' Staircase' comparison in *Un Amour de Swann* (see p. 103) above). In *Axel's Castle* (1931) Edmund Wilson devotes a long chapter to *La Recherche*, but the title and the central idea of his novel *I thought of Daisy* (1929) are a more telling tribute to Proust.

It is very probable that conscious influence underlies a quotation we have used from T. S. Eliot (p. 81–2). The connection made there between memory and imagery would bear out Proust's hope that his work might affect the sensibility of some who read it by making them aware of what was already their own – 'they would not be *my* readers, but readers of themselves' – (my italics). A further indication of the meaning and the fulfilment of this hope is the way in which later writers have found their own preoccupations reflected in *La Recherche*. Samuel Beckett's remarkable study (1931) has been mentioned (pp. 15, 39 and 44) above), with its intensifying concentration on the themes of grief and loss. Thus, too, Virginia Woolf, who from 1922 almost till her death often mentioned Proust's novel, spoke in a letter to Roger Fry in 1937 of the experience of 'vibration, saturation' it brought her, and added 'there is something sexual in it'. 'How at last has someone solidified what has always escaped before?' she asked, and a reading-list she composed for a friend in the late thirties contained the judgment that Proust was incomparably the greatest of modern novelists (from a letter to Margaret Llewellyn Davies). In contrast, D. H. Lawrence soon abandoned the attempt to read *La Recherche*, with the comment that it was 'too much water-jelly', while Henry James, who read *Swann's Way* soon after its publication (i.e. before the outbreak of the 1914 war) was enthusiastic enough to send its author a fan-letter.

The early history of Proust's reception by English-speaking writers is perhaps best represented by one who understood him to the point of wanting to undertake the immense task of translating *La Recherche*. C. K. Scott Moncrieff began on this in 1920 and it dominated the rest of his short life. Proust wrote to him from his deathbed, in October 1922, to praise the English rendering of *Swann's Way*, not without once more deploring the general title *Remembrance of Things Past*;

and added that he had not written to any of the other translators into several languages whose work he had seen. In a letter two months later, Joseph Conrad told Scott Moncrieff that the language of the translation seemed to him to surpass the original in mastery, but also commented that Proust 'enlarges the general experience of mankind by bringing to it something that has not been recorded before'. In thinking of the work of Scott Moncrieff, and of its painstaking revision by Terence Kilmartin and Andreas Mayor (1981), it is perhaps natural also to reflect on the immense extent of what we must call the passive reception of Proust by readers in many languages other than French – particularly Russian and Italian, as well as English – who have given no literary expression to their response, but in whose culture this novel has long been influential.

In German, one of the earliest and most sensitive of Proustians was Ernst Robert Curtius, whose brief and excellent article on Proust's writing (rather anticipating Auerbach's methods) appeared in English in *The Criterion* under T. S. Eliot's editorship in 1923. Curtius, and others, condemned the first German translation of *Swann's Way*, by Rudolf Schottländer, which came out in 1925 under the title *Der Weg zu Swann* (another misnomer). As a result of this a contract for the rest of the translation was undertaken by Walter Benjamin in collaboration with Franz Hessel, but of this only *A l'Ombre des jeunes filles en fleurs* and *Du Côté de Guermantes* were completed, and financial disagreements with a second publisher prevented more being done. Benjamin felt that Proust's writing was of such importance to his own concerns that it would be wrong to continue the work for inadequate remuneration. The nature of this concern was an intense preoccupation, from which there arose Benjamin's valuable essay 'The Image of Proust' (1929 in *Die Literarische Welt*, later collected in *Illuminations*) and a series of short pieces in Proust's manner written in 1932 and published as *A Berlin Childhood about 1900*. Proust himself advised the writing of pastiche as a kind of spiritual exercise or exorcism, for he felt that his own gift for mimicry, both spoken and written, made him liable to produce slavish imitations of authors he admired; his stylistic independence was to be re-established by propelling the salient traits of, for instance, Flaubert and Balzac into absurdity. The fragmentary childhood memories through which Benjamin explores certain philosophical ideas are rather imitation than pastiche of their model; they lack colour and light, and the interaction of the child-figure with adults is spectral where it exists. Physical experience is over-hastily indicated in these pieces, and gives way at once to metaphysical speculation. A very short example may be given in its entirety; it is called 'The Larder':

My hand stretched forward into the crack of the barely open larder door like a lover into the night. Once at home there in the darkness, it groped for sugar or almonds, sultanas or preserves. And as the lover embraces his girl before kissing her, the sense of touch had its tryst with them before the mouth tasted their sweetness. How the honey, the handfuls of currants, even the rice gave themselves caressingly to the hand. How passionate was this meeting now that both had at last escaped from the spoon. Gratefully and wildly, like a girl one has snatched from her parents' house, the strawberry jam let itself be enjoyed without bread and as it were in God's open air, and even the butter responded tenderly to the bold wooer who broke into its maiden retreat. The hand, the youthful Don Juan, had soon penetrated into every cell and fastness, with flowing strata and streaming masses in its wake: virginity, which uncomplainingly renewed itself.

More than one volume could be filled with an account of the echoes of *La Recherche* in France; it may now be taken for granted that anyone of modest literary culture will have read *Swann's Way*, at least. But we know that the early reception of the work was very much bedevilled by the circumstances of publication – obviously many who might have been enthusiastic readers were deprived of any hope of understanding the whole. An even more serious disadvantage at the outset was the reputation for short-winded 'elegance' Proust had acquired with the articles and stories he had published before 1913. Reviews of *Swann's Way*, with every allowance made for the preciosity and gush that characterised the literary journalism of the period, read like attempts to do as well as possible by a frail and deserving minor author who was also a personal friend of the reviewer – a line of faint praise which was used, incidentally, as a weapon by Sainte-Beuve in his time. Maurice Barrès was one contemporary who reflected, after Proust's death, that he himself had completely failed to understand what the then available volumes of *La Recherche* really signified for the genre of the novel. It is true that within a few years the general public response to *Swann's Way* was excellent, and that the jury of the Prix Goncourt recognised this by their award to *A l'Ombre des jeunes filles en fleurs* in 1920.

One of the most intelligent readers of Proust imaginable in France ought to have been André Gide. Unfortunately he was somewhat disabled by knowing Proust personally, and because they were both homosexual. What Gide insists, in his diaries, on referring to as 'uranism' formed the subject of their few conversations (they did not, apparently, meet between 1892 and 1916), and its treatment was at first the principal interest of *La Recherche* for Gide. 'You can say anything you like, as long as you never say "I"!' was Proust's advice, far from acceptable to the relentlessly truthful Gide, who had moreover already heard it from Oscar Wilde. To Gide it seemed a betrayal, for which he gently reproached Proust (see Gide's diary for 1916), that homosexual love was represented in *La Recherche* as dark, joyless and sinister, and its devotees as the victims of a curse. For Proust, as for Mlle Vinteuil, this moral attitude verged on a physiological need.

'A vague mixture of admiration and irritation' is Gide's reaction, in 1938, as he finishes reading *A l'Ombre des jeunes filles en fleurs*, which he had never got through before; and he also expresses a view close to that of Henri Ghéon's 1914 notice of *Swann's Way* in the *Nouvelle revue française*. It is, that the writing is the preparation for a work of art, not the thing itself, an edifice with the scaffolding still masking its architectural outlines. Clearly it took a long time to establish true receptivity to Proust's achievement, and this may be connected with what has been briefly said (p. 92–3 above) about the resistance the French tradition of lucid perfection offers to such a work.

In one odd respect Sartre's reactions to Proust emerge from a concern similar to Gide's, though expressed in a new formula. Proust's lack of commitment, whether to acknowledging his own homosexuality or to rejecting his bourgeois background, offends Sartre or is used as a pretext for condemning his work. An element of bias becomes evident, as is pointed out by Joseph Halpern in *Critical Fictions* (Yale, 1976, p. 74). Sartre was generous in his assessment of writing as a reflexive, self-conscious act, the 'invention of the self' – his own activity in his re-interpretation of childhood, *Les Mots* (1964) – but this generosity is not extended to Proust. Perhaps the challenge of *La Recherche* remained too disturbing to Sartre in his own account of how the child he had been turned into the writer he had become.

The recent generation of critics in France have concerned themselves with Proust in countless aspects. Notably, Roland Barthes's *Fragments d'un discours amoureux* suggests a further dismantling of the novel form, beyond Proust's perpetual 'work in progress', and in certain pages a consuming desire to have written that very work himself.

Critical works mentioned in the text

Auerbach, Erich, *Mimesis* (New York, 1946)

Beckett, Samuel, *Proust* (London, 1931)

Benjamin, Walter, 'The image of Proust' in *Illuminations* (Berlin, 1929; English edition, 1970)

Benveniste, Emile, *Problèmes de linguistique générale* (Paris, 1966)

Curtius, Ernst R., 'The style of Marcel Proust' in *The Criterion* (London, 1923)

Eliot, T. S., *The Use of Poetry* (London, 1933)

Genette, Gérard, *Figures* (Paris, 1966–72)

Halpern, Joseph, *Critical Fictions* (New Haven, 1976)

Minogue, Valerie, *Proust: Du Côté de chez Swann* (London, 1973)

Muller, Marcel, *Voix narratives dans La Recherche* (Paris, 1965)

Shattuck, Roger, *Marcel Proust* (London, 1974)

Sartre, Jean-Paul, *Situations II* (Paris, 1948)

Further reading

Works by Marcel Proust (with dates of first publication)

Les Plaisirs et les jours (Pleasures and Days), 1896
Preface to translation of [Ruskin's] *La Bible d'Amiens* [1884], 1904
Preface to translation of [Ruskin's] *Sésame et les lys* [1865] 1906
Pastiches et mélanges, 1919
Chroniques, 1928
Jean Santeuil, 1952
Contre Sainte-Beuve, 1954
Correspondance (ed. P. Kolb), 1970–83
Correspondance générale (ed. Robert Proust and Suzy Mante-Proust), 1930–6

Besides the three-volume edition of *A la Recherche du temps perdu* (Gallimard, Bibliothèque de la Pléiade, 1954) already mentioned, two further Pléiade volumes, published in 1971, contain *Jean Santeuil* with *Les Plaisirs et les jours*, and *Contre Sainte-Beuve* with the rest of Proust's shorter works. *Jean Santeuil* was translated into English by Gerard Hopkins (London, 1955), and *Contre Sainte-Beuve* as *By Way of Sainte-Beuve* by Sylvia Townsend Warner (London, 1958).

Critical and biographical works

a   Collections of essays

Barthes, R. (ed.), *Recherche de Proust* (Paris, 1972)
Bersani, J. (ed.), *Les Critiques de notre temps et Proust* (Paris, 1971)
Bloom, H. (ed.), *Marcel Proust* (New York, 1987)
Cocking, J. (ed.), *Proust: Collected Essays* (Cambridge, 1982)
Girard, R. (ed.), *Proust, a Collection of Critical Essays* (New Jersey, 1962)
Price, L. (ed.), *Proust: a Critical Panorama* (Urbana, Illinois, 1973)

b   General

Probably the most stimulating recent critical work on Proust is that of Gérard Genette, whose approach is flexible and various, and who is always leading or luring the reader back to the text. Genette's essays appeared in the three volumes entitled *Figures I, II, III* in 1966, 1969 and 1972; these are available in English as *Figures of Speech*, and the third volume, after an introductory survey of critical methods, is devoted entirely to the application of some of these methods to aspects of Proust's writing. For readers of the present study, the essay on 'Metaphor and metonymy' is likely to be the one of primary interest and the most accessible for a start. 'Proust as palimpsest' in *Figures I*, and 'Proust and indirect speech' in *Figures II* are also essays of great importance.

The secondary literature on Proust is now enormous — there were over two thousand items in French by 1939, according to Douglas Alden in *Proust and his French Critics*, 1940. We refer the reader here only to some works, many of them in English, which have stood the test of time, to some which are very recent, and for the rest to the extensive bibliographies available.

The following two German critics approached Proust through close textual reading; it is the tradition in which Erich Auerbach also wrote:

Spitzer, Leo, 'Proust's style' in *Essays in Stylistics* [1928] (English version, Princeton, 1948).

Curtius, Ernst Robert, 'Marcel Proust' in *Der französische Geist in Europe* [first published 1918; new edition, Bern, 1952]. This is a longer version of the *Criterion* essay referred to above.

The rest of the list belongs to the comparatively recent generation of Proustian criticism:

Brée, Germaine, *Marcel Proust and Deliverance from Time* (London, 1956). (This is a translation by C. J. Richards and A. D. Truitt of Brée's *Du Temps perdu au temps retrouvé*, Paris, 1950.)
The World of Marcel Proust (London, 1967).

Ullmann, Stephen, *The Image in the French Novel* (Cambridge, 1960). Proust is one of the four authors considered by Ullmann, and the chapter is of particular interest because the examples of his imagery are nearly all taken from *Du Côté de chez Swann*.
Style in the French Novel (Oxford, 1964). Contains a good many references to Proust and a chapter on his 'synaesthetic' imagery.

Poulet, Georges, *L'espace proustien* (Paris, 1963). Emphasises the importance of space in *La Recherche*, felt to have been critically neglected in the concern with time alone.

Rogers, Brian Goodwin, *Proust's Narrative Techniques* (Geneva, 1966). Looks forward to modern methods and is still very valuable.

Barthes, Roland, 'Proust and names' in *To Honour Roman Jakobson (Paris, 1967)*. Barthes sees the name, rather than ideas about memory, as Proust's starting-point.
Fragments d'un discours amoureux (Paris, 1980). Apart from explicit quotations from and references to Proust, there is much in this moving and almost testamentary work that suggests a close kinship.

Tadié, Jean-Yves, *Proust* (Paris, 1973). Very scholarly and comprehensive; it is a feat to have kept its length to 330 pages. It

takes into account not only biographical data, detailed year by
year (several pages each for the later years), but also Proust's
working notebooks (*les cahiers*) and early writings, to explain
the composition of *La Recherche*; it also summarises the work
of other critics. The select bibliography is to be recommended
for its useful divisions by type and theme.

Richard, Jean-Pierre, *Proust et le monde sensible* (Paris, 1974).
Approaches *La Recherche* through the study of sense impressions, with section headings such as 'velvety', 'dappled',
'spurting', 'fragrant', etc. Very spirited and original, though
the style seems of earlier date than the ideas.

Ellison, David. *The Reading of Proust* (Oxford, 1984). With
valuable chapters on Ruskin's importance for Proust, largely
original but making available to readers without much French
some of the previous work on this subject by (e.g.) Jean Autret.
This book is also remarkable for evident delight in its theme.
Critical theories of recent years are given careful attention, but
this is a very independent approach.

Henry, Anne, *Marcel Proust: Théories pour une esthétique* (Paris,
1981). The point of departure for this somewhat polemical work
is the period Proust spent as a student of philosophy and
literature (1894–5). Mme Henry traces the genesis of *La Recherche* to Schelling and Schopenhauer; Proust heard a course on
their thought by Séailles at the Sorbonne.

Proust Romancier: le tombeau égyptien (Paris, 1983). Connects
Proust's ideas on aesthetics with those of several German
thinkers of the nineteenth century and earlier, and asserts the
philosophical basis of *La Recherche* almost to the exclusion of
the literary.

Nemerov, Howard. *The Oak in the Acorn* (Baton Rouge, 1987).
Lectures given at Brandeis University in 1968. Exceedingly
relaxed and subjective, but notable as being addressed to an audience unable to read French, and consequently referring only
to the English translation of *La Recherche*.

Malcolm Bowie's fine inaugural lecture at Queen Mary College
(London, 1978) is entitled 'Proust Jealousy Knowledge', insists
on complexity, and though primarily concerned with Marcel
and Albertine in *La Prisonnière*, begins and ends with the
parallel situation of Swann and Odette in *Du côté de chez
Swann*.

c   Critical biographies, bibliography

Maurois, André, *A la Recherche de Marcel Proust* (Paris, 1949,
translated as *Proust: Portrait of a genius* by Gerard Hopkins,
New York, 1950). Still a stimulating and readable work with an

immense number of quotations from the letters and recollections of Proust and his contemporaries; despite its date, this biography has the quality of closeness to its subject in time.

Painter, George, *Marcel Proust; a biography*, 2 vols. (London, 1959 and 1965). Erudite and exhaustive on facts, strangely close to the method of Sainte-Beuve in interpretation.

Bardèche, Maurice, *Marcel Proust romancier* (Paris, 1971). Very thorough confrontations of Proust's earlier writings with *La Recherche; Du Côté de chez Swann* receives particular attention.

Bonnet, Henri, *Marcel Proust de 1907 à 1914* (Paris, 1971–6). Tracing the composition of the novel side by side with biographical events. In his second volume Bonnet briefly outlines the place of *Du Côté de chez Swann* within the whole work. This book also contains a useful chronological bibliography.

d Personal recollections

Duplay, Maurice, *Mon Ami Marcel Proust* (Paris, 1972). A single specimen of the many books by friends. This one is artless and unpretentious; its author knew the Prousts as a family.

Albaret, Céleste, *Monsieur Proust* (Paris, 1973). As told to Georges Belmont, a long and delightful memoir by Proust's friend and housekeeper during his last ten years. A girl from the country when she entered Proust's service, Céleste became his confidante, messenger and comforter, and gave proof of extraordinary gifts of tact, sensitivity and strength of character.

e Continuing serial publications

Bulletin de la Société des amis de Marcel Proust et des amis de Combray (Paris, 1950–)

Les Etudes proustiennes in *Les Cahiers Marcel Proust* (Gallimard, Paris, 1973–)

Bulletin d'informations proustiennes (Presses de l'Ecole normale supérieure, Paris, 1970–)

These periodicals publish reviews, bibliographies, articles, and new material directed towards Proust studies, and are the best indication of the response of the French reading public to their greatest modern writer.